LISA H.

a series exploring the intersection of life and loss

First edition

ISBN: 978-1-945962-27-1 (paperback)

Published by Lisa Hagan Books

Cover design by Inna Savchuk

From Death To Life:

The Incredible True Story of Anthony Joseph

Terri-Ann Russell

LISA HAGAN BOOKS

First I will introduce you to Anthony Joseph, aka "Butters" the second of my four children, who came charging into the world two weeks early on June 10, 1992. The glue between my two other sons and my daughter, he would say. From the beginning Anthony did everything like he knew the shortness and preciousness of the time given to him. He exited this life the same way at just 27 years old, in July 2019 -- died unexpectedly from a medical emergency. Suddenly he was gone, breaking our hearts with the loss, and just as suddenly he returned to share world-changing knowledge and spiritual truths from the afterlife. This book is about him and the message he is delivering to you through me.

Sometimes I refer to Anthony in the past tense but it's out of habit. He is still very much present, not just as a living memory but as a living consciousness, a person who laughs and loves as a spirit the same as he did when alive in his body. I hear him clearly in my mind and feel his presence. When I speak about him in these pages I do so with the sound of his voice in my ears. He is quite humble and bucks at his mother's praise for her amazing son.

From now on, as much as possible, I will refer to him in the present tense, as the living person he is, whose body died but he lives on continuing what he started as someone who cares passionately for the well-being of others and is on a mission to help. He wants to show you that life is eternal, love is unconditional, and humanity is leveling up to a joyful, new phase of spiritual life.

I think we should all learn to refer to our departed loved ones in the present tense, for they have moved on to a place where we all go eventually and are not gone. They are present with us whenever we open our minds and hearts to them. I will show you how I do it with Anthony and teach you to create beauty out of pain and grief, so the truth can be yours and you can share your life with the spirits of your loved ones and ancestors.

In his journals, Anthony speaks of himself as an old soul. His sensitivity and empathy weighed heavily on him -- he hated being an old soul. The energies of other people clung to him like soggy clothes, but despite the personal expense he still took every opportunity to help anyone suffering or needful.

As a June baby born under the sign of Gemini, Anthony was and still is a people person. Despite having a huge circle of friends, few people really knew or understood him. Even I, his mother, found him to be a mystery. He and I are quite different -- he is like a mirror reflecting back a better version of me I can and should be. Constantly surrounded by friends and loved ones, he craved time alone, especially when the bandwagon attached to him overloaded with the cares, concerns, and troubles of others. The two sides of his Gemini nature wrestled ceaselessly; he struggled to stay balanced.

People loved Anthony -- they still do, but when I use the past tense here I am referring to my memories of him before he transitioned out of his body. His ability to connect attracted everyone he met to his "humanness." He loved deeply and held those personal connections close to his heart -- and still does. While he could read people empathically and give them what they needed, he had difficulty doing it for himself.

He inspired everyone he met to be a better person and leave the world a better place. He walked his talk, too.

At his funeral we heard stories from Anthony's friends about how he would take them in and work to make their lives better, and even how he saved a friend's life who was dying in his arms. The community of Flagstaff, Arizona where he lived rallied around us, and people from all over turned up to pay their last respects. They all thought he was gone, but he was there with us on that terribly difficult day. I could sense and smell him everywhere we went.

His brother Erich summed up Anthony's approach to life while eulogizing him. Erich quoted something he heard a lot from Anthony: "Erich, don't be an asshole!"

We all laughed. That was so Ant. It could be the title of our next book. Imagine a book about spiritual life titled Don't Be an Asshole. He believed he would rather be happy than right, especially in his relationships with people. Assholes would rather be right than happy.

Anthony tells me this book is the first of three we are writing together. He has much to share from his experience alive with us and alive in the next life.

The relationship between Anthony and his brothers was unique from the start, beautiful and amazing and deeply connected. It solidified as time passed and they grew together from children to men. Anthony's childhood nickname, Butters, gave him the idea to call his brother Tyler "Toast" and his brother Erich "Jam." That easy sense of humor and quick wit is still part of him, even though he's no longer in his body. I hear him laughing as I write this, remembering those fun times with his brothers. He reminds me that he is never far away.

The Terrible News: Anthony Is Gone

Anthony is not here in the physical with us, and I am finding it very difficult to fathom. Strong emotions overtake me at moments. They roll in, they roll out, they roll in again like tumbling waves. Sometimes I wonder how I will get through the day without him, and suddenly he swoops in and reminds me: he is there -- no, he is here -- to guide and direct me. I can accomplish anything with him at my side. I tell everyone to watch and see what I do with this deep pain inside me.

But before the waves begin rolling ceaselessly, I experience a moment when the world stops. It freezes cold and solid as I hear the most devastating news of my life. My son is dead.

My son is dead!

Every emotion, every pain and every fear surfaces as I feel like I am going to vomit and faint. "How is this happening ?!" I scream. My heart rips. A pain so severe I cannot regain my senses. I remember listening to the officer explain how they tried to save my son but were unsuccessful.

How is this happening, is all I can think. A tunnel of stifling darkness forms around me. My ears still work; I can hear the officer, but he is at the other end of the long tunnel.

Distant. Unreal.

This isn't happening, this isn't happening, this isn't happening!

My body and mind feel separated. One stands on solid ground and the other floats high above in orbit, looking down at the planet and wondering if it's real or a mirage. A dream.

A nightmare.

Then I feel my son's presence.

Knocked flat by shock and sorrow, with the walls still closing in and threatening to pull me down to a place I might never return from, I feel a shift. My "angel ear" buzzes with a high-pitched sound.

A sign I'm about to faint? A symptom of shock? Tinnitus?

No, it's the sound of a voice speaking from beyond. Free of the body, the spirit can vibrate much faster. A clear, high bell singing joyfully. It's Anthony's voice but I can't decipher what he's saying.

I scream *Anthony's here! He's here! Oh my God he's here!*

Am I screaming out loud, or only in my head? Is it the wail of my breaking heart? At that moment it's all I can do to stop the pain, to escape the walls crushing me to nothing and leaving me there to die.

This really is happening. My son is gone, and just as quickly as he departed he's back again. Or is it more accurate to say he never left?

Anthony knew. He knew the shock overtaking me. He knew the danger threatening me so he came and helped me. The voice of the angel in my ear was his voice. In my mind, I only heard ringing, but in my heart I felt my son. I suppose a skeptic might say it was "all in my head," a coping mechanism, a delusion, a symptom of shock or even a psychotic break. But Anthony is my son. He grew in my womb for eight-and-a-half months and filled my life with his incredible spirit for 27 years. I know my son. He came to me during my hour of greatest need and lifted me with his feathery wings out of the tunnel of despair.

Later, after I settled into my new existence as a mother with a son who is a spirit that comes and goes from my presence, I learned that what happened the day he died is part of a soul contract agreed to prior Anthony and I incarnating on Earth as mother and child. He didn't decide on the spot to rescue me that day -- it was a contingency plan agreed to ahead of time.

We write this story of life together, outlining the plot before incarnating, then filling in the details as we go. In the outline of our story, conceived while in spirit, Anthony and I agreed that he would come into the world through me and we would live together for as long as he needed to finish what he needed to do, then he would exit. And if the loss was too much for this mortal mother to absorb, he would come to my rescue. And he did, thank God.

Now he tells me, *Ma, the story continues....*

The Soul Contract

The definition of unabridged is "not shortened; complete." After the funeral, Anthony told me the unabridged version of our soul contract. Very clear and to the point. That is my son even in spirit. Anthony is either very long-winded or concise.

The contract is completed, he told me.

His sudden departure was not an accident, he wanted me to know first. He had completed his cycle in this lifetime. Prior to birth we plan our lives and have contracts -- agreements -- that are detailed and specific. We decide when we are going to come in (be born) and when we are going to exit (die) and work out the details with other members of our soul group. Soul contracts have room for flexibility. For example, we are each given a number of points in a lifetime when we can exit. It's not written as a specific day and time. It's basically once we have completed our purpose for coming to Earth to live in a body, or have come as close to it as we're going to come. Then we exit.

Knowing this does not make my loss any easier. I simply understand better. It helps.

Anthony had a contract for his life, and I have a contract for mine, and together our contract is well-documented. He told me he had completed his contract and departed when the next exit point arrived.

These contracts are also in place so that the spirit can leave the earthly body if it indeed gets too rough here in Earth school. In Anthony's case, his work was done; he could leave. Without knowing all the details, I have been able to find out pertinent information from Anthony in our sessions -- yes we meet regularly. The first order of business: discuss our soul contracts.

Soul contracts. That might be a new term for you so I will explain it. When we are planning to incarnate on Earth, we work out the details with members of our soul group who incarnate with us in the body or remain behind to act as spirit guides. Angels are involved, too. The finalized plan becomes a contract (or think of it as an agreement) and an outline for how a person's life evolves. Earth school is designed to teach us, allowing for amazing growth as a soul during our time here. Life is not random, but our free will to make decisions can take us far away from our original purpose for being alive in the body and make it seem random. Each soul can decide with their soul group to incarnate or not. It is truly up to the individual.

The teaching experiences can be difficult and very painful during our earthly journey, but the rewards make everything worthwhile. The soul decides to incarnate to help members of its group with their life lessons. But they have their lessons too, and members of their soul group join them on Earth to help them learn. The contracts are never one-sided. They are multifaceted. We are always seeking to grow spiritually and help others in the process.

We each have an innate purpose -- this the first thing to understand. As souls we travel and experience life together both in body and spirit. Imperative to our growth as individuals is the journey of self and learning to navigate through life. Some heartache, some pressure and some good times are likely to come. Some souls choose to learn more difficult and painful lessons. Some have the ability to learn but are held back by their human limitations and unable to fulfill their mission.

The contract stipulates how, when, and where certain things must be done. Think of it as planning a trip with destinations in mind and flexibility for how to get there. As we move along the journey of life there are usually stumbling blocks to help us to awaken to our true self. Our true self is an expression of love and kindness. It knows no restrictions and lives life from the heart. Earth school lessons teach us and put us back on the path of embodying our true self.

One Soul, Many Lifetimes

We bring vast knowledge from other lifetimes embedded in our DNA and cellular memory, although much of it remains locked. Memories of past lives can be put to great use in our lifetimes now. We learn on our spiritual journey that indeed we can unlock this DNA and reprogram the cellular memory. We learn by navigating our self-development -- walking the road of life to our true self -- and begin to understand that growth is a sometimes painful but necessary process of learning lessons to help us evolve.

Some people choose to learn about their past lives through past life regression and other means. But everyone whether they know it or not is heavily influenced by their past lives. For example, the people in your life who push your buttons the hardest are often members of your soul group. And whether they know it or not, they choose to have these experiences with you to promote growth. Growth is fundamental for becoming the "you" that your soul knows you can be. It's why you carefully plan your life at the soul level. Without second-guessing the process, we as humans begin to evolve into a new form. But like a plant emerging from a seed, our growth can first require us to break through a hardened exterior.

Anthony's death broke me open.

The next phase often requires us to come to a balance in our Earthly experience. This balance is what many of us need to learn on a soul level. Before incarnating in a human body you are asked what you need to learn. Then your soul group gathers and helps create a detailed plan. Thus, you make your contract and they make theirs.

Some souls will choose a more difficult path to help them grow more extensively. Although the path is determined before we incarnate, we still do have free will to move about our Earthly experience our way. Whether we choose to learn the lesson or try again at another time is entirely up to us. But putting off our growth can mean later opportunities to learn a lesson are more difficult.

A powerfully stark and also enlightening realization emerges out of the information Anthony gave me in our first session: each of us chooses to come here to Earth to live a preplanned life. We choose to experience certain things and to incarnate with our soul group. Also, some souls learn many lessons in a lifetime, and each can be more difficult and painful than the last.

Connection with Anthony

I work as a medium, channeler, past life regression therapist, and healer in the wonderfully mystical town of Sedona, Arizona. It's famous as a place with special energy, and many people with special gifts and abilities are drawn there to visit, live, and work.

You could say I was prepared well for my son to visit me in spiritual form, but my sessions with clients work differently than my visits to the higher realm of existence where Anthony lives. I use a specific process for meeting with him, following his instructions. I begin with deep breathing, spiritual protection, and visualization. I bring myself up to the 7th plane where he lives, a dimension of existence "above" the physical dimension of space and time. He uses the analogy of a pinball machine to describe the process. I visualize a ball of light moving from my heart space to the 7th plane, and repeat it three times. Then I call in the white light around me.

As I visualize this pure, spiritual light spreading out, I begin to float across a gateway, through the portal of ordinary consciousness, and meet him on the other side. I visualize my energy spreading out until it encircles us. I know when he is there with me; I feel him in every sense of the word.

The emotions are powerful, and I use the energy to flow into my work. It requires unwavering focus and concentration, and the reward for my effort is I get to be in my son's living presence. I get to go where he lives and experience his reality, to ask him questions and know him more fully both as a spirit and as the son I raised.

Anthony usually waits for me to ask the questions when we meet on the 7th plane. There are other times throughout the day where he is just there with me. I feel him. Or I see someone walk by on the street or in a store and feel his presence, and I ask if he's with me. During those times, he visits me in my reality, the material reality.

As I begin to connect with Anthony on this particular morning soon after his death, my heart is heavy. I am longing to connect with my son and ask him many questions. He begins our communication:

This was not my human choice, Ma, but my soul's contract. As Anthony I didn't have a choice. My soul contracted this before it came here. Please understand this. I know you know what I am telling you. Everyone can learn something from my experience on Earth.

Teacher to the pupil, Anthony sits in a lotus position -- I see him in my mind's eye. It's such a weird experience to switch roles with him. I taught him everything I could as his mother. Now he teaches me.

Ma, feel into your immense pain. Let it engulf you fully. Call in God and the power of love to heal your broken heart. You must take time to retreat and allow your physical body to heal. Your physical cannot keep up with what's happening on a spiritual and emotional level.

There is a majestic path for every one of us. Sometimes it is a short path, as in my case. In other cases, a longer time is spent on Earth. Time does not equate to experiences lived or learned on Earth, it simply just is. What I learned on Earth I now carry with me. I've been here (in the next life) for only a little bit but have learned so much, it feels like forever in a sense. There is a process to follow here, a protocol for all souls to lift our vibration and heal from our Earth trauma.

No one is exempt from this process.

I am in a quick review of the necessary facts that I need to know right now, but I am learning that my mission here is profound, and I find it quite fulfilling.

I wish there were better words to explain it, as these words do not even come close to what I am experiencing.

I interject. "Anthony, I feel the same way, there are no words to describe the pain I am feeling. It's as if I have died myself."

I know, Ma. It is not an easy process to undergo, but please understand that I am there with you every step of the way. This was part of everything that we predetermined before we came to Earth together. I know everyone is having a hard time processing this loss.

If it helps you to know, again my human self did not want to leave. It was a shock to me as well. It took me aback. But once I transitioned and stepped through the doorway I knew I was home. I know this is little consolation when you are suffering such pain but try to understand, this was all part of a contract. My contract and our contract together. I am so sorry that you are all suffering in my absence, but please know I am never far away.

He goes on to explain that these contracts are set forth for us to spiritually advance in our lifetime. A returning to a remembrance of who we truly are as spiritual beings voluntarily having a physical experience.

As I feel his presence begin to leave me I am overwhelmed. I cannot understand how this has occurred and why I am here suffering without my son. As time goes on, I begin to accept that the suffering is not being done to me. It is facilitating much growth for my soul as I undergo this journey. And I chose it before coming to this world to live the story of Terri-Ann Russell.

The Story of Us

Our story begins long before the existence of Terri-Ann and Anthony. Our souls united many times and in many places across all timelines and dimensions. The story of Anthony and I goes deeper and further than what the human mind can comprehend. It is not just the story of us but the story of all of us.

We are all connected and have lived many lives before our current incarnation. Our soul family and interconnectedness to one another bridges the span of lifetimes. This is one of the main reasons Anthony is guiding me to write this book. Everyone who has suffered a loss needs to understand THE BOOK CONTINUES....

As Anthony and I contracted to be together in this lifetime we met in another realm and discussed coming to Earth together. Through past life regression I have since learned that it was a lesson for both of us to agree to the circumstances in this lifetime.

For me, I needed to go through the grieving process without taking my own life. I knew intuitively that I had failed this lesson previously, not fully recovering from a heavy loss in my life and instead I chose to exit. I agreed to try again to learn this lesson if I had other children who were dependent on me in this lifetime. I knew that I could not leave if I had a young child who needed me. I also knew I had to learn kindness and compassion as my soul wanted to advance further than it had in previous lives. So I agreed to this contract.

In my past life regression I could see and hear the meeting between Anthony and I. We sat together in a room full of books similar to a library, with many other souls involved in the process. Anthony agreed to be my son in this lifetime, but he was to leave early at age 27 to help me advance in this lifetime further than I have in other lifetimes.

We plot an agreement that would work for both of us. To join together as mother and son in this lifetime for our benefit and many other souls. Anthony also had growth lessons to learn in this lifetime. He was to learn forgiveness for self as well as teach unconditional love. We sealed the agreement and made our pact to continue to Earth in this lifetime as mother and son.

The conversation goes something like this:

Anthony: Will you come to join me in this lifetime as my mother? I may leave early if I can accomplish my goals in a shorter time. I will help you advance as much as I can while together on Earth, and help you advance after I am gone. I need you to teach me about unconditional love and compassion so I can teach it to others. I need you to help me with my growth as an individual, and I will help you with your growth.

Terri-Ann: I will agree to come in as your mother, but I need you to help me through loss in this lifetime so that I can understand what it is like to suffer a huge loss and remain behind and work through the process of healing while helping others who have suffered a loss.

Anthony: I will agree to that for you. I will come in as your son in this lifetime. but I am only staying for a shorter time. My cycle will be completed for what I need by age 27. 2+7=9. Nine is a time of completion, so I must do what I have to achieve by 27.

Terri-Ann: I agree but I must have support on my end and a young child that will need to be cared for so that I can stay and achieve my contract.

Anthony: I will make sure that you have support from me after I pass and support from others that surround you on Earth. I will help you to advance greatly while learning kindness and compassion from you.

Through regression we can look at past lives on this planet, as well as on other planets and in between incarnations. It can open us to a whole new world. I specialize in past life regression, and in my experience it creates a communication channel with the higher self and subconscious mind and supercharges spiritual growth.

Today as I write this soon after our first meeting in the 7th plane I understand more than ever the story of us, the story of Anthony and I and what we agreed to in another time and space, though as his mother in this lifetime, losing him is unfathomable. A time will come for acceptance but I am not there yet. Maybe by the end of the book I will be closer. When we lose a loved one, we lose something in ourselves that can be very difficult to find again.

I connect with Anthony this morning and immediately the grief and sorrow pour forth. "Anthony, please help me to understand this. I do not want to be here without you."

Anthony: Ma, You have to. You have to go on and persevere without me in the physical sense. What you do not understand yet is the infinite light that will grow out of this
darkness for you. We begin our lives long before we ever
incarnate in this life. This is just one small piece of our soul
essence, a predetermined life that we choose when we come
here.

What you do not understand is the magnificent impact that
you will have on others and their journeys as you begin to heal
your internal wounds.

I wish I could show you everything but alas I cannot. Some information will come in and you must digest it first like food for
your hungry body. Please know that I am never far away. I am
always close by. I know it doesn't feel like that right now but it
is true. Even if I am working in my world I can be in more than
one place at a time.

I can visit your world in a second. This offers a minuscule
amount of comfort when the pain you are in physically is so
substantial. I am sending you signs and communicating with
you daily through telepathy. This connection will intensify as
I help you unleash your potential.

The world I am in is perfect. I have never experienced such
beauty in my human life. It is peaceful and loving, something I wish your world could be. I know you are hurting
now and it probably always will to some degree, but please
know that I am forever with you and you are forever with
me.

My physical presence is gone but not forgotten. I'm in a place, almost like a dream-state, vast and huge that goes on forever as far as I can see. The colors are amazing and the music is nothing I've ever heard before. All of the beings around me help me and show me the ropes. I am home. I try to show up [in the material world] as much as I can without overburdening you.

You see, as far as you know, I am right next to you as I am doing my work. Here it is much different than there. It doesn't work the same. Light can travel faster than the eyes can see.

Transcendental meditation is wonderful for you now, Begin to do more hypnotherapy work and make more recordings of your sessions with me. Continue to work on yourself, Ma, you need to release some of this heavy pain you are feeling. Transcendental meditation helps to clear on all levels including the human psyche. It allows for miraculous healing as well.

I know it can be hard to keep your head above water now but reach out to me, please. Let me kneel before you and help you. I am here, Ma, My legacy and words live on through you. You must continue to share and bring to light what you know. I am here guiding you. I am here directing you; connect and follow what I am showing you.

You can easily flow like a cool breeze when we work together. It's as if I've never left you. I am with you more than ever before. No greater power than love, Ma, can you feel it? Can you feel me shower love and peace over you when you can't take it any longer? That's me. I wish you only knew the amazing benefits a hard human life can be when we cross over to this world.

The gifts that a hard life entail are even more beautiful, but you will understand that clearer as the process of grief and loss move along. I promise to allow you to do your thing, your way. I will not intervene unless you ask me to. I promise that I will always watch over you too, and the others. I miss and love all of you so much.

Please understand as much as you can, it was not my human choice to leave. As you travel with me on this journey we will embark on a road to beauty, love, and understanding. I will open you up to my world but you cannot stay.

There is no life without death, there is no light without dark, and there is no flow without hardship.

I love you forever and a day, Ma.

The book continues....

As my session with Anthony comes to an end I feel his presence leaving. It is overwhelming for me both when he comes in and when he leaves. I have done this work before but nothing compares to having a direct connection to your child, your flesh and blood now in spirit. I compose myself and begin to go about my day. By now I am learning to navigate small pieces of my life. I took care of my daughter today, so I consider it a good day.

We decided to take this journey together before we even incarnated on Earth as Terri-Ann and Anthony. I don't fully understand this contract and why I would have agreed to such a painful experience, but I begin to understand there is a higher power at play here. There is a reason indeed for why I agreed to such a contract, and it is part of my evolution of understanding as I navigate the remaining part of my life on Earth.

No one is here by coincidence, and the people that come in and share our journey are not here by coincidence either.

A Mom and a Medium

As a multidimensional healer and medium I am learning far more from this process of grief than I could ever imagine possible. I am being taught directly from Anthony (his personality) and his oversoul (I'll reveal more about that later). He will continue to be my greatest teacher and my son. Both aspects of him speak to me when I connect during our sessions.

I connect to be closer to him in the afterlife. I crave that one-on-one time with him. Understanding what has come to pass. Beginning to see a much deeper level of existence as Terri-Ann and Anthony. We are all in this together and intrinsically connected. When a human passes to the afterlife they require healing. Living this human, dense-filled life can be difficult, and when we pass we need time to recalibrate and heal. Those heavy things that we thought might have been important while on Earth are just life lessons for our true expansion as spiritual beings.

Without life in the body there is no death, and without death there is no life. So we incarnate many times, sometimes learning the same lessons over and over until we achieve balance. Why would one choose to come here? Quite simply, we come to Earth school to learn. We are all here to learn and grow then carry those lessons with us to the afterlife where we can put them to other use. Terri-Ann and Anthony the souls have been to school together in lifetimes previously and shall continue to do so long after Terri-Ann and Anthony the personalities move on. Our oversouls continue to seek expansion through countless incarnations of itself in countless times and places simultaneously.

What we know of ourselves consciously as human beings is like one facet of a diamond, and the oversoul is the diamond, the whole picture. All of us exist not only here in human form but simultaneously in other forms -- even in other times, places, and dimensions. The concept is so foreign. Words do not capture the dynamics. Most people must experience it personally.

My experience happened at The Stupa, a place famous in Sedona, Arizona for its cosmic energy. Meditating, I heard something begin speaking to me, though "speaking" is the closest word to describe the experience of downloading information and energy. What you "hear" is a translation of it to terms you can understand, and the source doing the "speaking" transmits thoughts and ideas.

At The Stupa I was given my soul name, and it became day one of a quest to understand what it meant. Is Terri-Ann my soul, Zahasra, or is my soul me? After months of pondering this I embarked on a deeper journey into transcendental meditation and again sought out my sacred space, The Stupa, and remained there with the intention to learn everything connected with my soul name. What transpired took me to another level of understanding. I was told that I am a transmitter -- I transmit energy out like a radio tower. I received many downloads that day, along with the following message:

You are me and I am you. There is no separation, though you seem to think there is. The oversoul (Zahasra) and the personality (Terri-Ann) co-exist.

Terri-Ann is free to go about and make choices while in Earth school, but ultimately Zahasra will guide her. So while you as Terri-Ann believe you have free will, you do for the most part, but your oversoul has the final say about things agreed to prior to incarnating in the body.

While this might seem daunting, the lessons on Earth can be heavy but not as daunting as you feel it to be. So in simple truth there is no separation as you seek to understand you are a piece of me.

I am Terri-Ann the mom of four children, one in spirit. I am Terri-Ann the medium and message carrier for a son in the afterlife. And I am Terri-Ann, a soul that planned this life in part so you can read these words and know these truths.

I DIDN'T SEE IT COMING

S oon after we found out Anthony had died I was showering and getting ready to drive two hours to the south valley to go tell my boys and my parents that our beloved Anthony had passed to spirit. I was showering and could hear him screaming at me... I'm OK, Ma! I'm OK!

The shock hit me. A glass wall separated us and he was screaming for me to hear him. I could only cry, "how can this be!!!" I was so distraught -- even breathing came with difficulty. He was trying to tell me he was OK but my inner ears only heard the dirge.

I was trying to hear him and understand but I just couldn't contain myself. My heart never felt such pain, and my brain said "nope," it would not process what had happened. The memories are a blur -- most of them are forgotten. At one point I felt myself leave my body. A piece of me protecting me from this immense trauma. Trying to understand the words... your son is gone, deceased. Trying to stay in a space of being able to communicate with him. But I was having a hard time understanding this myself. I could hear him yelling intermittently at me but I was not fully understanding yet. How could this be occurring? My son... gone? It was too much to bear.

On the car ride down, my husband drove and I connected with Anthony and asked him to show me how he died. I needed to know if he suffered if he had been in pain. Little did I know that this feeling would encompass my entire being.

It wasn't like a typical medium session -- for many years I had been a medium, and this time it was my child, my flesh, my blood. Nothing could prepare me for how overwhelmed I would become. I asked Archangel Michael to surround us both with light and protection. I felt urgency from Anthony, wanting to connect with me. He knew I would be a mess. I had just re-experienced the same stupendous loss of a loved one as I had in a previous lifetime, and in that life I decided to exit rather than bear the pain.

Anthony was already doing so much work and reaching out to many people in my life that are open to communication with spirit. As I arrived at my sons' home and at my parents', I would have to repeat the words again and again, "Anthony is dead."

These words still torture me. The worst feeling in the world coursed through me like a song looping back to the beginning as I was forced to repeat the words to my family. The news shocked my sons Erich and Tyler so hard they stood frozen as I tried to console my mother and father. My husband was at a loss. He felt helpless. Again I left my body, a piece of me floating separately as I tried to process all that was happening to our family.

I needed to know he was OK. I heard him say it, but was I really? Or was it wishful thinking? My mind playing tricks on me? My psychic senses blared "full alert!" Everything was happening too quickly for me to comprehend. I knew I needed to text my psychic co-workers at Sedona Soul Sisters, Rozlyn Reynolds, and Ivory LaNoue, for them to confirm that he was indeed OK -- it wasn't just something I wanted to believe.

I am very blessed to have such amazing people in my life. I was guided to Sedona Soul Sisters while meditating at the Airport Mesa in Sedona. I met with Roz and explained what I had heard while in meditation at the airport, and a few months later we began working together. Looking back now, I see a piece put in place for me to bear what was to come. The soul contract between Anthony and I included other souls who also agreed to be part of it. Roz and Ivory became part of my life just in time. It's no coincidence.

Anthony's presence remained with us while we gathered everyone and tried to understand what was happening. Our entire family congregated in my parents' home as we began to plan for what was to come. All I wanted to do was to hold my baby boy. But I couldn't. The morgue wouldn't let me see him until they released him to the funeral home. I was desperate -- I would not believe he was gone until I could see him.

My sons were devastated, no color in their faces, processing grief in their own way. And me, their mom, holding space for them to undergo this process of losing their beloved brother and barely able to function for myself.

My daughter Sophia was on vacation with her dad, so I waited to tell her when we met later that week in Flagstaff. She was so very close to him. I knew her heart would be broken in pieces. My stepdaughter was with her mom that week also, we would tell them both and bring our family together to say our final goodbyes to Anthony's physical body.

Sophia is still very connected, so I knew Anthony would be able to communicate with her. He tells me he visits her in her dreams often.

Roz and Ivory both confirmed with me that indeed he was OK and he easily crossed over. Although it was a complete surprise for him to be out of his body, once he crossed he felt at home. He said to Ivory, "I didn't see this shit coming." This was the message I had gotten as well. Just before he died he thought he just had a stomach bug. He visited an urgent care and was sent home with a stomach bug diagnosis.

In my experience as a medium I'd never connected with a spirit who had crossed so suddenly and unexpectedly then connect with a medium so quickly after passing. Most of my clients' loved ones have been in spirit for longer than three months before communication begins with me. I did not yet fully understand how Anthony was able to communicate so easily and so quickly, but Ant was just as amazing in human form, so in spirit form I expected him to be no different. I have heard of only a handful of people that were able to adjust so quickly like him. Ivory explained it just doesn't happen much, but he was able to do it.

A disjointed feeling hovered with me as the hours passed with my family after first hearing of Anthony's passing. In two places at once, somewhat here and somewhat there. Two worlds, one for the living on Earth, the other for the living in spirit. I felt Anthony come into my presence again. It engulfed my being. For my child to be communicating with me as a spirit overwhelmed me.

I begin to cry out for him.

And he begins to speak to me....

Ma. I am so so sorry that you are hurting. I am so sorry that I left.

I was just as surprised as you were. I was not sure what was going on. One minute I was in the room in severe pain and not being able to breathe, and the next minute I was being lifted out of my body. I was semi-floating in the room watching the paramedics work on my body. I felt as if I was still there yet I was not.

I watched and watched in dismay as I could hear them calling the time of my death. I was confused. Dan (Anthony's roommate) was there and he was extremely upset. I kept calling to him, "Dan I am not dead, I am right here." He could not hear me.

That's when everything changed. I was moving again toward a beautiful platinum bright light, floating away through a massive tunnel of light. I kept looking back to what was happening on Earth, but I was so mesmerized by this amazing light that I was fixed on following it.

I felt surrounded by familiar beings but not sure who they were yet. As I began to slow in my movement the light dimmed a bit. I could see a doorway of sorts. A beautiful gateway to the oneness I was becoming.

I felt like a feather and in no more pain, but I mourned what I was leaving behind. I could still feel an immense connection to all of you, and yet I wasn't sure where exactly I was. You see, Ma, I was loving the feeling of the light but sad for leaving you all. I knew you needed me to be there, but I couldn't stay with you.

We agreed to this before we became me and you. Some things are just too hard for you to understand right now. There is an innate process that you will come to understand when you leave your human form behind. On the Other Side I was met by beautiful light beings and familiar faces. Great-grandpa and Benny are here with me. And grandma too. They were waiting for me. Many beings. All sorts of energy that felt familiar. I felt safe and secure as I made my way home.

I know this is a lot for you to comprehend at this moment but I want you to know that I am OK right now. I didn't mean to leave you, Ma, I could never leave you guys behind. Please tell everyone that I love them and I am always going to be there for them. I promise to connect with you often, and I will make my presence known to all of you as much as I can. Please do me a favor and let Dan know that it's OK. He did what he could.

This message would come through again later, repeated by a medium I used to work with in a small boutique in Sedona. Dan was Anthony's roommate for many years after they met in college. During the time of Anthony's passing Dan expressed his concern for Anthony, but neither of them thought his "stomach bug" was anything to worry about. At age 27, who thinks they are going to die?

Back at my parents' home, we began to talk about the plans that we would have to make. My husband Tim took the reigns and immediately began calling around and connecting with people in Flagstaff. Word spread quickly. Erich decided it would be best for him to go up and stay with Dan, considering Anthony died in their apartment. Dan was very distraught and we knew he needed us there with him as well.

The time raced by as we had some heavy decisions to make concerning the arrangements and how we were going to handle everything. Erich really stepped up for me. I could not have done this without him. He knew everything about what Anthony would want, and Erich and Tyler discussed funeral arrangements. Anthony was very particular about many things, but if anyone knew him best it would be his brothers.

The police detectives were very helpful, explaining how the system works as they tried to unravel the last few days of Anthony's life. A detective in Flagstaff intuitively felt Anthony's death was related to a medical condition, and that's also what I felt. The coroner's office in Flagstaff was also very supportive.

I wasn't really there during this whole process -- part of me had floated away as an act of self-preservation. I shut myself off from the details. The officials explained things as best they could, but this is my son they were speaking about. I just could not understand how all of this was happening.

Something in me broke and I wasn't myself. I knew it, but I couldn't stop from being taken over with dark thoughts and evil forces.

I was going to join my son.

I could not bear the pain.

There was no doubt in my mind where I was heading. I began to hear thoughts about wanting to kill myself, and malevolent entities laughing and taunting me.

I would cry and scream for the son I had just lost and the voices would get louder. I would get myself so worked up I could not breathe, and then my son would step in. I would feel love and peace encompass my entire being and my breathing would slow. He was there every single time I felt I couldn't go on without him. His spiritual presence would enter my space and I would hear his voice coming from outside my body:

Ma, under no circumstances, are you to follow me. The trajectory of a disaster would be great. Many lives would be affected. You cannot follow me. No matter what. Trust me on this. You must stay behind, no matter how much it hurts!

His strength got me through that moment, but the voices returned later, the dark things chipped away at my defenses, and I'd find myself again staring into the blackness.

THE DARK ENTERS

Nightmares.

Nightmares so intense you can't make it up. Dark thoughts and impulses. Dark entities, their voices taunting, *"Kill yourself, you can be with your son...."*

During the first month after Anthony exited I fought to stay alive, to resist the urge to end my life and go find my son in the afterlife. You might not think it is a long time to be under the influence of dark forces, but they quickly took me over, and I needed help from a higher power. Anthony guided me to ask for help.

Me? Ask for help? I find it as difficult as he does. By that time I knew his exit from life was part of a plan, a contract, and in that contract I agreed to stay on Earth. But between overpowering grief and the dark things that entered my dreams, I could no longer fight the good fight on my own. I asked for help. Angry and full of hatred, I could not mourn my son and fight the dark forces that were attacking me.

My Sedona soul sisters, Roz and Ivory, put a protective barrier around me. A friend, Ed, gave me orgonite tower busters (a mixture of orgonite and crystal that clears harmful EMF and other types of energies) and an orgonite pyramid to keep under my bed. It helped to keep away the darkest of the dark, but the intense nightmares persisted.

Night after night the dark things would enter my dreams, keeping me awake and trying to break down the protective barrier. They knew my intense grief and never-ending pain and came at me from all angles. I would try to rest and they were there. I would try to meditate and they were there. There were fighting with guns ablaze and I was going to be taken over if I didn't fight back.

You can be with your son as soon as you want to be. Do it, do it, kill yourself!

I would be walking with my daughter and hear clearly, Jump in front of a car. It'll be over quickly. He's waiting for you.

"No!" I would yell.

Torn. I wanted so badly to be with my son, but suicide was not the way. If I killed myself I would have to come back and learn this lesson again. I'd leave behind family and friends I love, and the loss of me would rip them up. There is no guarantee I would be with him in the afterlife, either. I knew that.

The sibilant voices of the dark things spoke to me. They found my weaknesses and exploited them without mercy. I really needed help. It was all I could do to fight back and stay sane.

I pray to be able to sleep safely and undisturbed, but the dark things psychically attack me in my dreams and waking life. And just as I start to think all is lost, Anthony taps me on my leg sticking out from beneath the bed covers. It makes me smile, knowing I am safe and he's there to protect me and help me fight this fight.

Each of us is suffering in our own way. I cannot understand how anyone else feels because I am still trying to process my feelings. But I am mad. I am mad that the dark can even think about taking me over.

I am grieving my son and have to fight the dark. It seems so unfair.

"I am fighting to stay here without you, Ant!"

The darkness hears me cry out for my son. They are watching, ready to descend on me when I fall even deeper into the low vibration of grief.

I scream out for him again in my sleep, "Please Anthony, help me!"

I wake up at 3:11 a.m. He's here with me, I can feel him in the room, watching and protecting. Sending energy to radiate my entire being. He is trying to help me raise my vibration so I can fight the dark, but I am weakened. I want to run away, yet there is nowhere to hide. I see him in my bedroom, a shadow of light. I get up and begin to write.

He speaks to my mind and heart:

Ma, I am here. It's simple: if you flow, I flow. There is no separation. Connecting to me daily creates an impenetrable cord of flowing energy from me to you and from you to me. Bridge the gap to connect us closer and closer together -- our worlds will meet here.

I hear you calling out to me in your dreams. I am putting up as much protection and light around you as I can, but you have to do some deeper and intense work on yourself to help as well. I can feel your pain, and while you think that I might not understand, I do.

It's time for you to allow this flow of energy to enter you on a soul level. I will help you not only to amplify your healing but your entire existence. Feel the immense power within your being when we are connected. That's me and you. I'm in your corner whenever you request help or need something. I feel your feelings. I think your thoughts. We are connected....

I feel his energy fade away, and look at my phone. Almost 5:00 a.m. Time just flew by. I am tired, I must rest now.

I lay back down to sleep and the dark things pounce. They enter my dreams. They gnaw and pull me into a pit of despair. I scream out. Let the fuck go!

Poof. They disappear.

I feel myself returning. The dark entities can try all they want to bring me down, but I am far too full of fire energy to go willingly. Yes, my heart is broken and my life will never be the same. This pain is so intense. But I will not give in and be taken over. They will not take me down. I am a fighter. I have waged this war in another lifetime, as my son told me, and learned the lesson in the adage: this, too, shall pass.

I am attacked intermittently during the next few weeks. In time I gain my strength and begin to understand this new relationship I'm having with Anthony, but nonetheless the grief is still heavy in my heart. The darkness continues to pound at my shell, making it hard for me to come to a place of peace. Running on a hamster wheel is what it feels like, running and running but going nowhere.

I'm still not sleeping much or eating much either, but I'm gaining weight. It defies logic but I think I understand: Grief is so heavy and weighs so much on your nervous system. The system shuts down, and getting it started again is a big and seemingly endless push against inertia.

I wake up one morning with a heavy feeling looming over me. I can't get out of bed. Just making my daughter breakfast requires all my strength. I am upset and crying, not comprehending how this is even possible. The grief is an ocean with no bottom. Words cannot capture what has happened to me for the past few weeks. It's too much. I'm tempted to give in and say goodbye to this life.

I feel Anthony's presence and begin weeping.

Ma, open to the profound awareness that you exude through this human shell. Allow yourself the gift of light as you process these deep emotions. I will not let the dark take you over, but you need to help me in the process of protecting you. I can only do so much. It has to be you. Get in your warrior stance. Fight like you have never fought before. Stand your ground!

Remember who you are and where you came from. Fire energy engulfs you, and you understand that this fire burns deep within you. I know you have it in you. You need to dig deeper than you ever have. There is much riding on this.

You don't have a choice. It seems unfair but it has to be done and you have to do it. You guided me, now let me guide you. Trust me as I lead. You learn and I teach. Nothing could have prepared you for what is to come like these past few weeks have been preparing you. The warrior inside you is waging war with the dark. You know your power, and they know your power too. But they also know your weakness and they are coming at you. They will use whatever they can against you and get to you any way they can.

Tim (my husband) and Sophia (my daughter) are prime targets; watch them and add extra protection around them. Ma, you cannot be defeated, it is too important for you to win. You have waged this battle before [in other lifetimes]. Please understand it is necessary for you to accomplish this mission in this life, at this time. There is no continuance without you. Understand that. You must continue to fight to stay here. I know the dark feels all-encompassing, but you are making great progress.

Our bond is everlasting, Ma. We are working together to create this unique gift to the world. The worlds of matter and spirit *are coming together through our effort. Our worlds intertwine as one, and it is a battle. It wages within ourselves. That is the battlefield, Ma. That's where you make your stand against the dark.*

No one is exempt from this. We learn we grow, we expand and we move on to another dimension. I just experienced it faster than most. I have watched you wage this battle before and you will come out on top. You got this lady... trust me.

I feel his energy fade away, and I look at my phone. It's almost 5:00 a.m. Time flew by. I am tired and must rest now.

I am coming back to myself. I know that the dark can try all it wants to bring me down, but I am far too full of fire energy to go willingly. Yes, my heart is broken and my life will never be the same. This pain hurts so intensely. I will not give in and be taken over. There is no way for the dark things to get to me. I am a fighter. I have waged this war before as my son told me, and I will never go willingly.

Over the next few weeks, I am attacked intermittently. I gain my strength and begin to understand this new relationship I'm having with my son, but nonetheless the grief is still heavy in my heart. The darkness continues to pound at my shell, making it hard for me to come to a place of peace. I continue putting miles on the hamster wheel, running and getting nowhere. I'm not eating or sleeping much.

I sit and try to connect with Anthony, having a difficult time hearing him as usual. When he speaks to me it comes in like a shortwave radio, sometimes clear but other times muffled and going in and out.

I center myself, I can hear him.

Ma, you've got to do this. Follow me through the darkness. I am leading you every step of the way. Remember who I am. I told you we would get here. You must communicate my words through you to help others on their path of healing.

Growth comes from such pain and circumstance. You may not understand this now but ultimately you will. Not only will my voice help people to heal, but your voice will as well. Together we are unstoppable. Think of it as having a direct line to the universe. Guiding and lighting the path for you. LET ME GUIDE YOU.

The dark is seeking to destroy you now, they know you are at your weakest. Please hold your heart and let me hold you in the light. I am coming to you daily to help you persevere. Without you there is no continuance. You must understand this.

You must share your light with others in this lifetime. People want to hear our story and understand that death is just a word. A release from the physical being that keeps us chained to our personal narratives. Our souls live on in another dimension. Everyone can learn from what you are going through now.

Watch and see how you can grow from this.

You understand that our worlds are intertwined, but even know-
ing this you are suffering the loss of my physical being. It was
just a vessel to house our life together in this period of time. One
of many; we have lived many lives before. We are one, together.
Never apart, though I know it feels like it right now. You see the
hologram [the projection of higher dimensional reality onto 3D
space and time] and you understand. Hold on, Ma, a shift is com-
ing. I got you. I love you, and I will never leave your side.

I come out of my trance lightheaded but more at peace. "I will
continue to fight," I say aloud, making sure the dark hears me.
I have a higher power at my side helping me, and I refuse to go
down.

Before Anthony passed, I never had a problem keeping my vibration up. I did my morning spiritual practice to help clear
and ground me before working with clients. I took measures
to make sure I was protected from lower vibration energies
throughout my day. I always took time to meditate on what my
body, mind and soul needed, and I followed the guidance that
came to me.

It was interesting that I was having these adverse side effects of
being in that lower vibration. I was having trouble lifting myself
up from that level. Grief is such a low vibration.

Dr. David Hawkins, author of Power Vs. Force: The Hidden
Determinants of Human Behavior, is a pioneer in the study of
consciousness. His map of consciousness [see below] shows
where grief is on the vibration scale, below anger and fear,
graphically showing how grief can be badly damaging. When

your vibration is low, dark things that vibrate at low frequencies are able to get into your energy field, causing numerous issues and bringing out alternate personalities. It happened to me.

The light is beginning to return to me once again, though, and I yearn for a routine. And I'm finding it. Regular practice of connecting with higher sources such as spirit guides and divine love through meditation is allowing me time to heal. I began Reiki self-healing to help me move the stagnant energy that is sitting in my chest. My heart is so heavy, at times I feel like my lungs weigh a hundred pounds each. Energy healing is moving the energy from my body, allowing me to breathe easier and connect more clearly with Anthony.

Raise your vibration, Ma. Lift your frequency.

He too has gifts to share. His life is a gift for me and everyone who knew him.

Now, you can know him too.

RETURNING TO THE LIGHT

A few mornings after Anthony led me out of the darkness, I awoke to a new reality. "You shifted," I heard in my mind as soon as I woke up.

My soul sister Ivory texted me that morning saying she had heard the good news through "the grapevine." People with psychic and intuitive gifts know things without needing to be told the traditional way. Subconsciously, everyone is interconnected and able to share information telepathically. Ivory knew what happened to me overnight. A shift toward transcendence is a transformative experience, and it's good news worth sharing.

"What a gift I have been given!" I think to myself. The light is returning to my body and soul again after I thought it had been extinguished. Tears fill my eyes and grief presses heavily on my chest, but the despair of Anthony's death is lifted.

I remember the loss of my beautiful son as I do every morning when I wake up. *I hear him say, you did, Ma.* I held on through the darkest night of the soul and resisted the overpowering urge to end my life. I am beginning to understand that my son is always with me, and I can take solace in knowing he is by my side daily and directing me.

He is such a strong guide. His presence on the other side is felt by many people here on this side, and they share with me their thoughts about what an amazing soul and high-level being he is.

I decided to post to Facebook a picture of him laughing with his cousin Lisa taken during the previous Christmas, a ghost of Christmas Past. I can't imagine how we will ever manage to get through the coming Christmas without him here with us physically, but I am grateful for last Christmas and all the 27 years we celebrated together. And unbelievably, undeniably, he is still with us spiritually.

He says to me:

From pain to peace, Ma, you shifted.

What a beautiful gift you were given to be able to move through the darkness. It was imperative that you did. There will be times when the dark wants to reemerge within you still. Do not let it. The dark things haven't been defeated, but you must focus on bringing what you want to fruition, not what you don't want.

Keep looking for and following the breadcrumbs, I am sending you. Know it is me guiding you. I am reaching out to all your friends that I know are open to receiving me. You need the support from myself and others to navigate this road in this lifetime.

We contracted so much, please try to focus on the time we shared together and not the time apart.

Ma, there is no greater force [in you] than me and you together. Our soul has done many miraculous things over our lifetimes as other personalities. And this is not our final curtain call.

I know the pain can feel overwhelming at times, but call on your angels and call me in to help heal all that is needing to be healed. Ma, you must immerse yourself in the light. Follow the light to the people I am sending you. Keep seeing the signs -- they will take you where you need to be.

After our connection, I lay down to rest. It takes so much out of me. I read somewhere that grief is exhausting, not just physically draining to the point of being unable to get out of bed, but mentally and emotionally. Now add on the exhaustion of connecting in spirit with my Butters with the day-and-night war I fought against the dark things. Add on the continuous headaches from crying so much, and severe chest pain and sleepless nights with many painfully traumatic scenes looping in my head. For months the perpetual drain of flight-or-fight took a toll on my body, mind, and soul. Mom needs a good rest.

My shift toward ascendance is a turning point. The pendulum is swinging the other direction. The light is returning to my body.

Map of Consciousness Levels

from David R. Hawkins *Power vs. Force*

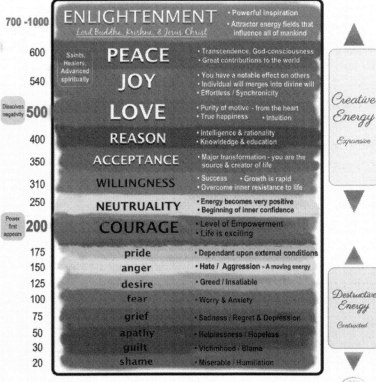

700 -1000		ENLIGHTENMENT *Lord Buddha, Krishna, & Jesus Christ*	• Powerful inspiration • Attractor energy fields that influence all of mankind
600	Saints, Healers, Advanced spiritually	PEACE	• Transcendence, God-consciousness • Great contributions to the world
540		JOY	• You have a notable effect on others • Individual will merges into divine will • Effortless / Synchronicity
500 Dissolves negativity		LOVE	• Purity of motive - from the heart • True happiness • Intuition
400		REASON	• Intelligence & rationality • Knowledge & education
350		ACCEPTANCE	• Major transformation - you are the source & creator of life
310		WILLINGNESS	• Success • Growth is rapid • Overcome inner resistance to life
250		NEUTRUALITY	• Energy becomes very positive • Beginning of inner confidence
200 Power first appears		COURAGE	• Level of Empowerment • Life is exciting
175		pride	• Dependant upon external conditions
150		anger	• Hate / Aggression - A moving energy
125		desire	• Greed / Insatiable
100		fear	• Worry & Anxiety
75		grief	• Sadness / Regret & Depression
50		apathy	• Helplessness / Hopeless
30		guilt	• Victimhood / Blame
20		shame	• Miserable / Humiliation

Creative Energy Expansive

Destructive Energy Contracted

NOTE: A person may operate on one level in any given area of life. An individuals overall level of consciousness is the sum total effect of all levels.

A New Life with My Son in Spirit

Anthony sends me so many signs. They are a map to get to where I need to be. The shift I feel is something intuitively I knew was coming but had no idea when it would arrive. It arrived right on time.

Every morning I ask him to guide me, and he lets me know what I need to do and where I need to go. I have been asking him to help me return to the light since he passed into spirit. I hear him say, "Watch the video, Ma."

What video does he mean? I pull up Facebook and there it is, a video of Tom Zuba speaking about Gary Zukav and the book The Seat of the Soul. I had run across it three months earlier but never got around to ordering it. After Anthony's passing, once again I was guided to purchase it so I did. As the video starts playing I look to my right and there's the book on my nightstand.

"Synchronicity, or what?" I say to myself. (Synchronicity is a term coined by Dr. Carl Jung for describing when a coincidence is meaningful and not random.) Anthony chimes in.

Or what? Total synchronicity, Ma! Remember the breadcrumbs? I am leaving them everywhere for you to pick up. No mistakes, no accidents, no coincidences. Only synchronicities! Why do you doubt me? You were made for this. I am here with you always, death cannot separate us. Without you, there is no me. Without me, there is no you.

Have you gotten this backwards? I am always here. Never apart from one another. A stone cast into the water, our love con-

tinues to ripple out through many dimensions. Unseen or un-heard to others but to us it is a constant. Secure and unob-structed we connect through many dimensions. Our worlds are intertwined.

Take your time, Ma, there is no rush. Feel me envelop your body with the light. It is returning to you. You are learning to house more light within you. Do not be afraid. Evil lives in the fear. I could never leave you, please understand this. I know you think that I do not fully grasp what has occurred, but I do.

I see your pain, your suffering. I am working to let it all unravel so that I can help you transition to the highest level of abundance while still on Earth. Please know that through the ages we are always together. Death is a mere obstacle and never a deterrent. I am more with you now than in my human life. The light will con-tinue to flow to you in mysterious ways. Allow for it all to come in. Light brings more light. Release the pain and bring more light into your body so you can flow to me easier.

I am watching. You are doing great and I am right there with you in this.

I'm out,

Ant.

Just like that he is gone again. I sit there in awe, having a hard time understanding. My brain is still very much in denial of his absence, yet he is right here with me every step of the way. Guiding and protecting me on this journey that I feel like I never would have agreed to, yet I am finding out that I really have agreed to it and even arranged to have everything needed to survive the ordeal.

Spiritual practice daily and focus on the present. That's how I'll get through this.

I am learning to navigate this uncharted ocean and bring peace to my pain. This endeavor is by far the hardest of my life. Even knowing what I know about the spirit world and the connection I have with it, my son's absence physically is an open wound. We will spend Christmas without his laugh and infectious love for life. Nothing can compensate for that. Loss is loss.

As I prepare for bed that evening I ask Anthony to come to me in my dreams. I have yet to have a dream visit from my baby boy. I want a dream visit more than anything. I'm determined to bring him into my dreams by filling my body with spiritual light. I am trying to get back to who I was before he transitioned, but the process to this point has been one step forward, two steps back. I set my intention and fall fast asleep.

The morning approaches quickly and I awake remembering that I had connected with him in my dreams. I run to get a pen and paper so I will not forget what it was about (a preparation I should have made before going to sleep). In my dream, Anthony is dressed in all white, his long hair beautiful and flowing. He is laughing and happy. We are at his funeral. He is mingling with everyone. I am like an outsider just watching him from afar, in disbelief that he is here and everyone can see him. He comes up to me looking healthy and happy and begins talking to me.

Ma, You'll never guess what happened? I was trying to put my hair in a ponytail and it snapped and ended up in my ear. I cannot get it out. Can you help me?

Without speaking, I move closer, still in awe. I grab and yank the ponytail out of his ear. He laughs.

Haha (with that deep belly laugh of his; I can hear it in my head as I write this)   DO YOU UNDERSTAND NOW? The grief was blocking you from hearing me clearly. My voice was muffled. It came through sporadically, now you can hear me clearly all the time.

You shifted. I knew you could do this. Communication shall be clear and precise from now on. You will hear me more often and just like I am there with you. I'm with you all the time. I will be talking up a storm to you.

Still baffled that he came to me in my dream -- my first visit in a dream with him since his passing, lying in bed, I connect with my higher self and hear:

"There is still so much that you need to learn. You are achieving a higher level of consciousness now. A deeper understanding of what has occurred and on a more profound level.

"The connection between you and Anthony shall increase your vibration as well as his. Even in death we are doing our work (evolving and expanding) and our vibration is increasing. It is not like on Earth where your vibration gets depleted. Here the energy exponentially expands and increases as Anthony goes through his own process. You are beginning to see and understand light and fibers (of spirit) through interconnection.

"Go deeper into your meditations. Your light is returning but be aware of the dark still trying to enter. Your battle has not ceased; there will be more hurdles for you to overcome, and you will begin to understand that there is never one moment without Anthony in it from here on out. He is with you everywhere."

I am beginning to understand that all I have learned up to this point has been nothing until the moment that I lost my son in the physical. While understanding that such a loss is extreme, it has a deeper and profound meaning that there are no words for. Anthony visits and communication helps me to open to the immense light within me again.

There is a higher purpose guiding all of this. While life without my son in the physical is the most difficult thing I have endured, I am learning that this immense connection is what is keeping me afloat.

I can never fully show the gratefulness and appreciation for the fact that my son and I have this connection of love that transcends time and space. I am slowly learning to navigate this journey with a newfound awareness that after death the connection is still there, and although it is a different relationship, it is a much deeper one

I have so many feelings of loss -- they can be overwhelming. Writing this book is helping me heal through some of my pain while navigating the grief journey. I am learning that grief is a process and it is one of many lessons life can teach us.

According to Anthony, we are given a cage that is to be understood as a gift. We unwrap what he means coming soon in the next chapter.

BREAK FREE OF YOUR CAGE

I write in a cage I did not build but I was GIVEN.

Anthony Joseph, 2016

I know my son as a spirit through our sessions and his continued presence in my life. Through the journals he left behind, I know Butters as the son I raised and a man of deep convictions and secret thoughts. The journals help me see some parts of him I did not fully know while he was with us physically. He was something of a mystery even I could not fathom.

What did he mean by a cage he did not build but was given? I wanted to know after reading that in his journal. By this point in the journey of losing my son then regaining him in ways I could not have imagined, he'd become ever-present in my mind, so I asked about that and a lot of other things, and here's what he said:

The cage is given to all of us. Unbeknownst to us at the time of inception, we are to break free of the cage (our limitations) and open up to a new existence.

[We're] not here to be punished for anything we do or have done, but to grow and evolve as a being. Our light shines through us for all those who are open to see. The dark tries to make it seem like the light will never win, but that battle has been going on forever.

I ask, "when does a person cease to exist?"

When your time is up?

Your physical leaves, but your true self never does. When your time is up your soul expands [out of the limitations of the human body], and love lives on.

There is no greater gift than learning while in Earth school how to create a new existence for your souls. Life on Earth is only the beginning.

Ma, time is in your world linear. But in the larger reality I know now, time is not limited by your linear conception. Viewed from where I am, all human struggles are fights against the constraints of space and time. Allow it to just flow free, to expand your breadth of life and breathe into your soul space to understand that there is only this moment.

I am forever with you on this journey and never, ever will leave you. Please lean on me when you need to. Expand and grow to your potential. We organized this before we came here [to Earth]. You will succeed.

Break free of your cage

Forever to eternity.

Ant.

Like last time I fully connected in the 7th plane with my son in spirit, I am blown away by the amount of energy that it takes. I am drained after our session.

Although this work in higher planes of reality is not new to me, having a connection with your child in spirit is taking time to get used to. Connecting with such a high-level spirit is overwhelming. I take in enough light to keep my vibration up and learn to house as much energy as I can. The lessons I'm learning from him are supercharging my growth and painting a clear picture of what a cage limitations are.

In my next session with Anthony, I ask again about the cage -- last time I asked he didn't give much detail.

Ma, the cage is given to you at birth when your limitless and immortal spirit enters a limited and fragile human body. The limiting continues as the first lessons in life center around what you can and cannot do, and further when you are told what you should and should not do and can and cannot be. You are taught to think certain ways, believe certain ways, and act certain ways, and these are the bars of the cage. Its lock is our inability to free our mind from the limitations. Most people do not know what life is like outside of the cage. They don't know their potential. Thus, they don't know they live in a cage.

It's like asking a fish what water is. Because it lives in water, it doesn't know there's a world outside of it. To a fish, water just "is." To a human, limitations just "are." They're facts of life, unquestioned assumptions. But question those assumptions and see beyond them and the scope of one's perceptions expands. Suddenly, you know no longer live in a fishbowl. You live in an endless ocean, an infinite universe offering endless experiences and expressions of life.

Our spirit fights tooth and claw our entire life to break free from the cage. It knows the reality it comes from before entering a human body and remembers its true power. Some people think they are happier in their cage and glad to be in it. They embrace their limitations and deny their greater potential. Life is more comfortable and easier to manage that way. But some people want to break free.

We can stay in the cage or we can move out, it is entirely up to us, but the cage is a given. And the cage we are in can be influenced by our life on Earth. We create a plan for events of our lives to help us get to where we need to be, but many times "life" can get in the way, ultimately keeping us locked in our cage.

It is almost as if there are two personalities at play, the free-roaming one that lives beyond limits, and the one that lets the cage dictate how life unfolds. It is an internal battle to bring ourselves to the point where we can break free from the cage, or stay within its limits -- limits that are self-imposed and self-perpetuating.

At times we might feel as if the cage has been opened up for us to run free. Then it is ultimately locked again, keeping us trapped in a cycle of trying to break free. It is all part of our evolution.

To the person reading this, it may resonate right now that you are fighting this eternal battle, wanting to be free but stuck and conformed to what society deems to be the correct way to live for you. Understand that you are not alone.

To eternity, Ma.

I love you,

Ant.

As I am writing in a light hypnotic trance, I feel his energy dwindling. Again, I begin to weep -- I wish I could live up in the ethers all day. I feel so at ease and at peace connecting with him. If I could turn back time and have my son back in the physical....

The grief process is so overwhelming, and the only thing keeping me here is my son in spirit.

I am experiencing a dark night of the soul as I am awakening to who I truly am and why I came here. My purpose is bigger than I could have ever imagined. Having my son guide me from spirit is hard. I want him here with me, alive in body, but there is nothing that I can do to change that. Joining him in spirit is comforting, though, and keeps my head above water. I wish my entire family could experience him how I am experiencing him on the 7th plane. They are all distraught and grieving. His death wasn't that long ago. So much has changed since then.

Fight to break free or remain within our limits. Life on Earth can make us forget who we truly are. I see glimpses of it when

I visit Anthony in his reality -- he is expanding and becoming a much greater being, and that being was there all along within him while he lived with us in the body.

Many of us are not ready to experience what we need to in order to grow. We have been indoctrinated to believe that only some of us contain the power to connect when in actuality all of us have intuitive this intuitive ability and others. By nature of our spiritual being, we all have the capability. But this human shell is a tough exterior, and to break out of it requires a shattering experience known as a dark night of the soul. A shattering so deep we have no choice but to wake up.

I call it a reawakening. A remembrance of what you truly are. Remember and you can break free of your cage, whatever that cage is for you. The cage of limitations is created from the same blueprint for everyone, but we make it our own, and the longer we remain in it, the more it becomes all we know. Can you break free? Some can, some won't or cannot because they don't tap their inner power to do so. Others choose not to see what is right in front of them, otherwise, they will be forced to change.

Breaking free of your cage requires much strength. You have that strength in your spirit. Going through an experience like mine is not required of everyone. I designed it for me, knowing how hard-headed I can be and how I had failed it in a past life. But think of other stories of enlightenment and reawakening we know from history. The Buddha broke free and awakened by sitting under a Bo tree for seven years, requiring amazing strength of will, yes, but not the shattering loss of a child and a weeks-long merciless attack from dark entities bent on de-stroying him.

The road is never easy. They say the greater the reward, the greater the risk, and the reward for passing the tests and shifting your consciousness to a higher level is beyond measure -- but the degree of difficulty is up to you.

KNOWING ANTHONY JOSEPH

THROUGH HIS JOURNALS

When alive in the body and experiencing all the dramas of human life, Anthony showed his true spirit in his writing. He is a writer at heart, and to read his words is to see what was inside him all along -- something no one, not even his mother, knew the full extent. Reading his journal brings me closer to knowing the person he is and was.

I'm still reeling with this loss, though. Stepping away from the 7th plane and opening my eyes to the reality of life without him here on Earth punches me in the gut every time. Then I hear his voice in my mind:

Ma, stop fighting this!

I cry out, "I am trying, Anthony!" The pain is just too much to bear. I cry myself to sleep.

The next morning the sound of a door slamming awakens me. No one is home except me. No windows are open and the dog is in bed with me.

"I am up!" I say.

I hear him chuckle....

You are now.

My son, the friendly ghost. As a spirit his power has grown to be able to move objects in the physical world. We call it telekinesis, and more than a century of experimental science has proven beyond any doubt that it exists and you don't have to be a spirit to use it. But we are conditioned to doubt its existence, to accept the limits and remain in our cage like the good prisoners most of us are. Anthony no longer has such limits.

He knows how to get my attention, too, that's for sure. He always knew how to manipulate or work me, as he would say, and says in his journal that he knew how to get what he wanted, not necessarily what he needed.

I brew a pot of coffee and return to my bed to continue reading his journal. He was so deep and philosophical; I get lost in his words. He begins to write about being a Gemini and what it means to him. He struggled with two minds in one body, typical Gemini. As I read, I can feel him sitting on the bed, watching me read and cry.

He writes like he's having a conversation with himself, "Two minds, one soul... (or maybe I'm wrong; maybe one soul with many personalities). Fight it all you want. I will drag you down with me. If you let me. This cage was given to you. It should be viewed as a gift. If you view it as anything else it will drag you to the depths of hell.

"Why must you fight it?

"If you go peacefully without kicking and screaming, the breakthrough will be much less futile for you. But yet you continue to fight.

"Why? Control? Dependence?

"I don't know. I am just a guy, riding the wave of life, flowing to my soul and I am doing it my way.

"I let go, I win. I fight, I lose.

"When will I ever learn that without the fight there is peace. Flow. Essence. Energy. The mere things that keep me in the cage are the things I must let go of to be free of the cage.

"I know I can do this. I have to do this. But I am tired.

"Will it get easier if I don't fight? You are telling me it will, but ultimately will it. It is up to me right? Or is it?

"How can I further my existence and get to where I need to be in the form I need to be in while not losing who I am at the core. I fought hard to try to get there but ultimately maybe I am just destined to fail.

"I won't though...

"You know why?

"I have my mama's blood running through my veins. My God, if you knew my mom you would understand!

"She can chew you up and spit you out if you cross her, otherwise she will love you till the end of time.

"Tyler is a lot like her. I admire both of them greatly because I wish there was part of me that could do that.

"I know that I can face my demons and come out on top. Isn't that what we all want, just to break free from the cage? We all have demons, my demons are no different than anyone else's. We each just wear a different mask [over what we are inside].

"I have had my hardships and my triumphs. If I had to choose an age that I have been at my happiest it would be right now, at this moment in time."

Reading about Anthony's inner battle makes my heartbreak all over again. My son needs to be here with us. He's gone and there's nothing I can do.

I hear him say, Ma, your heart... Healing needs to be done. Go see Sedonah. You can't keep going at this pace. She can help you.

I will see her soon. And our healing sessions will be exactly what I need, just as Anthony says. But I'm still eyes-deep in his journal, and more people are coming to me to share their experience of knowing and loving my son.

An Old Soul in a Young Man's Body

Anthony's letter to his first love, Kristin, written while on the cusp of 15 years old, takes my mind back to that time in 2007. She and I remain close, and she sent me the letter. Young love packs so much emotion and experience into a relatively short timespan. He and Kristin shared a love of writing and more, an immense bond which had grown over the course of many lifetimes. A textbook definition of "soulmates." Of course, we didn't know at the time how the soul nature of their relationship elevated its significance, or that Anthony had 12 years left to live on Earth, adding urgency and potency to everything he did and experienced.

Shakespeare didn't just tell a story, he spun tales of operatic drama. Anthony didn't just live life, he juiced it for all the sweet and sour it could offer.

The relationship between him and Kristin was a growth relationship -- they came together to grow and expand personally and as a couple -- and its end after two-and-a-half years impacted him hard, as you'd expect such a loss to affect a young man after his first time in love. The experience brought us closer as mother and son, and we talked extensively about relationships. It's easy to think a 15-year old is just getting to know the highs and lows of romantic love, but he was way more advanced than I knew at the time. Now I have his letters and journal, and it's apparent to me how his life unfolded in ways to teach him all it could in the allotted time.

Anthony overflowed with knowledge. He did not fully under-stand it at his young age, but the old soul in him shows itself in his main outlet for his thoughts and feelings: writing. There, he talks about remembering things he couldn't trace to what he experienced directly or learned in school or elsewhere -- I suspect it was the old soul in him speaking from a much deeper perspective. Anthony craved to know everything he could. He loved school, and I don't know many parents who can say that about their child.

Most of all, Butters loved his "fam," a circle that includes his biological family, his soul family including people such as Kristin, and the extended family of friends he widened with every day he lived and every person he met. He was born knowing that his relationships were going to be the most im-portant part of his life, and his gigantic heart had room for all of us.

At age 17 he talked of a time when soon he would be on his own. He thrived in places where he knew he could do his best in the world. Anthony and his brothers grew up in a post-card-esque Victorian town called Hackettstown, encompass-ing 3.7 square miles of lush New Jersey landscape surround-ed by state parks, forests, farms, and quaint townships. Their sheltered life made Hackettstown a home in the deeper sense of being a place where they nourished, flourished, and be-longed. They were like plants growing in the perfect combi-nation of rich soil, sunlight, moisture, and TLC.

But Anthony was destined to expand his circle and horizons, to seek adventure and life in the mountains he eventually found in northern Arizona. He talked about being at home in the mountains and forests. The fresh air enveloping his soul, bringing him back to center.

He did not know the vastness of his being at that time, I don't think.

Anthony and I talked freely about life. We shared some of the same ideals and values -- a thirst for life, love of learning, and connectedness with our family -- but vastly different life experiences. From the minute Anthony was born he was an individual, an adventure-seeker.

And his greatest love was and still is for his friend-family in Flagstaff. He spoke openly of them, and I know he was at home there. Anthony would bring you into his fam and it meant everything to him. They shared a code of honor and mutual respect, and looked out for and cared for each other. An expression of the small-town values Anthony carried with him when he left Hackettstown, and of his inner nature. The wider world can seem impersonal and chilly when you are just a drop in the ocean of humanity, but within Anthony's family circle everyone was personally welcomed and warmly cherished.

Cycles of Life and Love

I read Anthony's writings and realize how his life taught him so much in a short time, and how the big wheels of his mind and soul turned slowly while the wheel of his life spun quickly. Everything he experienced distilled down to lessons he took with him to the 7th plane. There, as spirit, his human life fertilizes a growth process even more amazing than what I witnessed as his mother on Earth.

Cycles... rotations... interconnection and interrelatedness. These are soul lessons, and while on Earth Anthony began incorporating them so that he could"hit the ground running when he entered the next life. Keep in mind, he started communicating spiritually with me and other people he knew only a couple hours after his passing, something heard about only in cases where advanced souls are well-prepared for the transition. But Anthony died suddenly, unexpectedly.

Where Anthony is now, time works differently than the linear perception of time we experience on Earth, and in that sense we can't measure it by the same standards of what is quick or slow. But there is a body of knowledge about the afterlife, and by that standard Anthony is exceptional. It shows in his ability to immediately become comfortable and balanced in his new state of being as a spirit without a human body and begin using his new gifts.

Think of the examples we have of musical prodigies when they begin playing an instrument and in no time are astounding listeners with their virtuosity. They must have begun their learning long before what's inside of them is expressed musically, and it is much deeper than skills such as knowing how to read music or to make pleasing sounds with an instrument. The lessons that make Anthony a spiritual prodigy were already part of him when he stepped through the veil and once again found himself at home. True to his nature, he began expanding and using his gifts right away for the benefit of everyone he loved.

In the following passage from his journal where he talks about the 12th rotation and the cycles of life, he shows the spiritual lessons he was learning before he'd even graduated from high school. He was a 15-year old putting into words the messages that came to him through his soul and originated outside of material reality.

The Twelfth Rotation

The clock strikes with an ominous blow.

Listening to the pendulum swing back and forth.

As if each swing is a cycle

another time at its end.

Yet another to begin.

The complexities of the known universe.

And the unknown.

Similar to that of such a small sound.

A never-ending amount of matter and knowledge seeming to beat at a death-defying tone.

So simple.

Yet. So complex.

Why?

To see the world passing by.

Slowly.

Fast.

Not at all.

The power of the mind seems to cause so many things at once.

At times.

None at all.

Or perhaps.

Something in between.

But the middle is a fairy tale.

A neutral moment in time where all else is in balance.

Maybe that is the unachievable goal you wish to have.

Possibly already accomplished.

How to remember?

You cannot.

It is not able to be done.

For the clock beats a new tone.

A new swing.

But the same old pattern.

To predict.

But not to be surprised by a new form of your perceived world.

No power on this Earth will achieve this.

You will swing back.

You will swing forward.

But you cannot have both at once.

Impossible.

Maybe you can.

Already the tide changes.

The air flows anew.

Take it in.

Then let it go.

To fall into the space we call our own.

Are you there?

Or are you here?

Where?

Everywhere?

No.

You are not anywhere.

Because your perception is limited.

You see the road ahead of you.

The monotone of the pendulum is your solemn anthem.

Will it stop?

I cannot answer for you.

I watch my clock.

It is still.

No sound.

I will sit and wait to see if you may understand.

My mind is in tune with everything.

Yet nothing at all. My world is hidden. My universe.

Within a little box. I call my mind. Yet. The universe.

Contains my world.

Containing my mind.

My clock shall not strike again.

Harmony engraved into my thoughts. To think. Freely.

Restrictions die.

Immunity.

You cannot feel what I feel.

Nobody can. But. Maybe. You can.

Until you see a world. Where the sun may shine. The clouds may form. The rain may fall.

Lives are born. Lives are torn.

The beauty of the night. The chill of the winter.

The sweet smell of the flowers. The days pass. The days go back. The days' stand still. A world.

Where I crawl. I walk. I run. I sit. I lay. I sleep.

I am exiled.

From your world.

You are exiled from mine.

Because I think different. You think the same.

I think better. I think worse. I think nothing at all.

A piece of Eden. Within everything. Within nothing.

It does not exist. Maybe. It can.

That is for you to find out. For you to find out.

I will wait. For that. I am certain. Only for you.

****

I finish reading that passage and it sinks in, but I am confused about exactly what Anthony means. I need clarification, so I ask to connect with him -- it's a perk of having a child in the after-life who is readily available for communication.

I begin my meditation and instantly the feeling of love engulfs me. I begin to weep uncontrollably. The feeling is still overwhelming for me. I am learning to allow it to come to the surface and bring much-needed healing to me.

I sit and wait for the crying to subside, and I hear him. Today he is sitting in front of me, lotus position, long flowing hair and beautiful brightly shining eyes.

He is outlined by that beautiful glow. His presence is growing. He is advancing quickly, as am I.

I can feel the immense power of the presence I am in. This is my son but where he is now, on the 7th plane and beyond, he is a high-level being with a secure connection to me in this life.

We begin.

Why do you continue to cry, Ma?

I am right here with you. I have never left, from the very moment I left my Earth body behind I was here with you. I am never not with you. Do you feel me? That's me, Ma. My life force runs through your physical being. How amazing is that?

This energy that we are beginning to share when I enter your body is highlighting areas that need to become lighter. You are learning to house more light in your human form. While not everyone is capable of doing this, you are. This is why we are starting slowly.

I know it can be intense on you. Trust me. This is not something we have ever been able to experience before in other lives and is only possible in this life because of the immense work you have done to progress in this time of ascension.

I ask, Anthony, can you tell me about the 12th rotation? What does it mean? Did you know you were going to transition at a young age? Was this a premonition? Does it have to do with cycles? Twelve months? Twelve cycles of life? Was this a channeled writing piece that you did at age 15 without knowing what you were doing? Twelve years from writing this you would leave this Earth.

During the 12th rotation I wrote it. I guess you can say it was channeled writing. At that time I had no idea what it meant. Writing took me to a place that is not able to be described with words. Sort of like when you write this [book]. You are channeling me and turning pure thought into words.

You see, Ma, I watch. I listen. And I learn. As much as I am teaching you, you are still teaching me. Please know that. Again, there is no separation.

It was a premonition. Now I can see clearly what it was, then not so much. I just wrote what came to me.

We are all connected, and our lives together this time around are not just about you and me but what we can do in the world to be of service to others. The time of the 12th rotation makes sense when you think of it as the culmination of a cycle of lives and soul experiences. Reread it. See the deeper meaning between the lines.

There are parts that can help you unlock the knowledge deeply embedded within you. You need not wait till you die to decode anything. The here-and-now is present within you, and yet it seems too far off, doesn't it?

Let's decipher it together:

The clock strikes with an ominous blow.

Listening to the pendulum swing back and forth.

As if each is a cycle.

Is another time at its end.

Yet another to begin.

Here I am referring to time in other places and dimensions. Unbeknownst to me at the time, I had extensive knowledge of other universes through dreams. I could see time in other places and I feel there was so much more out there than we are led to believe.

You must be ready to step into those areas -- alas, I was not ready. Hell, I could barely step into my own area in those days.

Death and rebirth are one continuous cycle, without one the other fails to exist. Sometimes -- most times -- we must die in order to be reborn. In your case, it is figuratively dying; the part of you that holds you back must die and allow the fierce warrior spirit within you to fully come through to accomplish your mission on the planet.

I am at your side helping you to advance greatly. As my clock struck no more, I was taken to a place where my clock would strike again. I knew, Ma, my higher self knew. That is why I lived the way that I lived.

The complexities of the known universe.

And the unknown.

Similar to that of such a small sound.

A never-ending amount of matter and knowledge seeming to beat at a death-defying tone.

So simple.

Yet. So complex.

At that time, I was unaware of my telepathic abilities. I was able to sometimes hear and know things that were indistinguishable to others. I had a high-tuned perception to sounds. It is like my ears were tuned to another frequency. I could hear voices and sounds which sometimes were obnoxious. I remember wanting it all to stop. At times it became too much, so I smoked weed to help me relax and take down some of the octaves, down to a level where I was able to understand more clearly. Then I would write what I hear coming to me from other frequencies, dimensions, and realities.

These octaves could send me into a tailspin if I let them. Eventually I began to just roll with it. At age 15 what did I know though?

Why?

To see the world passing by.

Slowly.

Fast.

Not at all.

The power of the mind seems to cause so many
things at once.

This reference has to do with the 12th rotation. There is a specific reason there are 12 hands on the clock. We base our understanding on tangible evidence of time. Time does not exist though. Everything is happening simultaneously. Time passing slowly or quickly is a creation of the mind and feature of human existence. Existence as pure spirit is very different.

Therefore, [while in human form] we cannot always know the true nature of what is occurring. Those of us who are awake might seem mad in a world of beings that are asleep to what is happening in and around them. Damn, that world is hard where you are. Many things happening at once and then bam, nothing at all. But "nothing" is everything, and within us is everything there is, the entire universe and beyond.

It is a learning process to come to where you need to be while you are there [on Earth]. There is an innate purpose in each of us. A purpose to find our way back home [where we originate spiritually].

I am rambling now. Sometimes I forget that this [knowledge] is considered quite simplistic in my world. We do not use words here. Words are a human construct. They are limited.

We communicate telepathically, thus when you learn to communicate with others the teachings of spirit and divine love it will be through your intuitive senses. Teaching others how to use all their senses [known as "clair senses," discussed in a later chapter] greatly increases their ability to perceive and grow beyond their limitations.

At times.

None at all.

Or perhaps.

Something in between.

But the middle is a fairy tale.

A neutral moment in time where all else is in balance.

Maybe that is the unachievable goal you wish to have.

Possibly already accomplished.

How to remember?

You cannot.

It is not able to be done.

The middle is a fairy tale, a life within lives, a layover in the human body to help your soul advance. The fairy tale may not always be a fairy tale but instead, feel more like a nightmare.

Look around you. Many are awakening, and they are living in fear, not understanding that their soul is speaking to them, yet they are beginning to awaken to the divine within. A place that can only be accessed when the human and the soul come together as one. Not everyone can get here because of what they have endured in their life. Because of what they have been conditioned to believe, and what they still choose to believe long after they are able to think for themselves and know the truth that speaks from within them.

How to remember?

You cannot.

It is not able to be done.

For the clock beats a new tone.

A new swing.

But the same old pattern.

To predict.

But not to be surprised by a new form of your perceived world.

No power on this Earth will achieve this.

You will swing back.

You will swing forward.

But you cannot have both at once.

This here refers to the new perceptions of life you can gain as a person. It is merely a change of scenery if it does not occur within you; the pattern will remain the same as always. The pattern is hard to break as a human that has been indoctrinated to believe certain things throughout their lives.

The power on the Earth has shifted. When I wrote this, the power could not even be conceived to be changed. Many of the beings that had returned to Earth since I came here chose to leave at this time to guide from the other side. Not only guiding their families but helping their families to guide others in the process.

You are one of many that have chosen to be part of this mission of change. You are on the transition team. The time has come for your people to open to the light within them. How? By understanding we are all connected, and by understanding that the innate power lies within us.

Impossible.

Maybe you can.

Already the tide changes.

The air flows anew.

Take it in.

Then let it go.

To fall into the space we call our own.

Are you there?

Or are you here?

Where?

Everywhere?

No.

You are not anywhere.

Because your perception is limited.

You see the road ahead of you.

The monotone of the pendulum is your solemn
anthem.

As *humans we understand ourselves in reference to others. The conditioning begins at birth and continues throughout life unless you allow for reference to your only true self, the one within who guides you daily. Without it there would be no you.*

So *you ask then, who am I? You are you AND you are me, there is no separation, we are one -- we are ALL one.*

Understanding this simple statement is difficult for the human mind to digest, but it is already proven by your physics. Humans like to overanalyze and overburden themselves with figuring out things that just are and need no explanation.

Peace in the quiet. This peace brings the reference point for knowing you are never really here and you are never really there. You just are. Does that make sense? [Physicists call it quantum nonlocality; everything is connected or "entangled" with everything else not only in space but in time.]

To some it will make sense, to others it will coast over their limited mindset.

You, like everyone, have your own frequency that is yours alone. It's your anthem, the octave of your soul. No other person that exists has the exact same frequency or makeup. Encoded in your DNA, this anthem sings to the beat of your soul. Without it, there is no you. Take the time to find what this anthem is and how you are to use it in your world.

Will it stop?

I cannot answer for you.

I watch my clock.

It is still.

No sound.

I will sit and wait to see if you may understand.

My mind is in tune with everything.

Yet nothing at all. My world is hidden. My universe.

Within a little box. I call my mind. Yet. The universe.

Contains my world.

Containing my mind.

My clock shall not strike again.

Harmony engraved into my thoughts. To think. Freely.

Restrictions die.

When you understand what I am saying here, you will understand that the human perception is much different than the spirit perception. When I speak, I am not speaking through the mouth, I am speaking through my mind -- a facet of the vast mind that contains wherein the universal language of all light beings. Telepathy.

When we find harmony in our thoughts, we find peace within our souls. A remembrance of who we are at the core of our being. Free, brave. Freedom to be brave in this human world is a difficult concept for you as humans to understand. Not everyone is born speaking their truth. We hide, we shut down and we do not allow our true self to come through. Your restrictions die as you find your way back to who you truly are on a universal level.

My clock did not strike again -- the cycle of my life completed and my time on Earth would soon be done. I knew, Ma. I now see clocks as a countdown for others' earthly lives. I can see your clock and I understand when you will arrive [back home in spirit]. I will gather, and I will wait for you.

Immunity.

You can not feel what I feel.

Nobody can. But. Maybe. You can.

Until you see a world. Where the sun may shine. The clouds may form. The rain may fall.

Lives are born. Lives are torn.

The beauty of the night. The chill of the winter.

The sweet smell of the flowers. The days pass. The days go back. The days stand still. A world.

Where I crawl. I walk. I run. I sit. I lay. I sleep.

I am exiled.

From your world.

You are exiled from mine.

Because I think different. You think the same.

I think better. I think worse. I think nothing at all.

Although quite existential, this passage is a whirlwind of my mind at the time. Making known the unknown, the meshing of two worlds. The soul has a plan before it incarnates to try to experience as much growth as it can while on Earth. You may not understand all that exists now but you will. It will build upon the newfound awareness of what is to come in your world. The world is as it is. We wake, we sleep, we work and we exist, but there is so, so much more.

A piece of Eden. Within everything. Within nothing.

It does not exist. Maybe. It can.

That is for you to find out. For you to find out.

I will wait. For that. I am certain. Only for you.

Eden has been mentioned several times when you and I have connected, but it's not the Eden that you were taught. Eden is our true home, within everything and within nothing. There is only one space that exists and that is the space of the soul within you.

Eden where we will all meet again. A place of true blissfulness. A place like no other. Many books and scriptures suggest there is an Eden, and there is one [but it's not a physical place, it's a spiritual place, and it is found within you]. Know this powerful information you receive now, you can visit there with me and it will help you to understand more.

You are stardust.

I am speaking here of all of us finding out our true spiritual nature, some sooner than later. I knew on a subconscious level the extent of my soul and what it knew. While I did not understand on a human level, the soul guided and spoke to me, writing passages like this all the time.

Fifteen years old. It is hard to comprehend. At age 15 he had this immense knowing within him and would not truly understand it until he passed. As he grew into an adult it began to show itself to him more, but very few times did he speak about it. As I said at the beginning, being an old soul was a burden he carried.

I think it scared him to know things. It scared him to know that things would come to an end here for him. You'll see. In the next chapters of this book I will share with you the premonitions and dreams from his journal entries.

As deep as we've gone already, we have only begun. Hold tight.

THE DARK STRIKES BACK

I'm drowning.

The waves of pain and sorrow roll in and pull me under until I fight my way back up and gasp for air. I'm fighting to stay above water right now but part of me wants to stay under. Is it wrong of me to want to join my son where he is, in a place where pain like this does not exist?

The dark water of grief fills my lungs and I yearn for freedom. Freedom from this heavy body and heavy life. Days like today the pain is so great. Every cell in my body is exhausted. I want to surrender and just drift away with the tide into the never-ending sea.

Grief is all-encompassing: physically, mentally, emotionally, and spiritually. Grief is complicated, too, and I'm just beginning to understand it. Unless I can get control of it somehow, I feel like it will swallow me whole. It's supposed to change and ease with time, but I feel like it will never end.

The dark things have returned like sharks circling a tired swimmer. Merciless. Cunning. Waiting for me to give up. I'm fighting to stay alive. I fended them off previously, but now their attacks are breaking down my wall of protection. I am tired. So, so tired. I was able to get back on my feet for a while and rise above the low vibratory frequency emanated by the dark things, but they chipped away at my defensive wall, leaving me vulnerable once again.

I push them out and they find a way back in. Recently it happened with a client seeking spiritual help. A young girl came to me for an entity removal, and like me, she was fighting to stay alive, to resist the urge to exit this world. Her mother brought her to me, desperate to help her daughter. Whoa! I have never experienced an entity this powerful and attached to such a young girl.

I know the ramifications when I do this work without my frequency being up to par. It's potentially dangerous. To remove the entity I needed guidance from my angels and a much higher power. As I worked to remove it from the girl, I called in Archangel Michael and the highest angels to surround both of us. I had to raise my frequency enough to stay in that particular zone as I blasted the dark thing with light. I called in Anthony to enter my body and give me the power and protection to remove it from her. It zapped every bit of energy I had. But I was able to remove it, and the young girl left feeling lighter and more positive about her future. Her demeanor changed and she looked different from the girl who walked into my office that day.

Then: more clients, more entities, more battles between the forces of light and darkness. The dark things came after me and my family again. My frequency plummeted and I had difficulty raising it back up to where it needed to be. My family was also under dark attack -- the dark things are relentless in their pursuit. A skunk attacked our dog, my daughter injured her collarbone, and my husband is having nightmares.

It didn't stop there. Intense outbursts of rage from my mother. My son's tires are going flat weekly, without rational explanation. These might seem like minute things to the normal person, but dark attackers take no prisoners and go after everyone in my circle. It is up to me to put up massive amounts of protection for myself and my loved ones.

Worldwide, the dark is losing this battle and fighting talon and fang to overthrow the lightworkers and get back on top. Prior to Anthony's passing I could do this work safely because of my ability to keep my frequency high enough to keep out the dark. But after months of constant battle, I need to take time off from work and focus my energy internally. I can see what is happening, but do I have the will to keep going, to keep fighting? I'm not sure.

And the attacks continue. While driving to work today I get an eerie sense that I am not alone. Darkness descends on me -- this has been happening sporadically over the past few weeks.

"Go away! Leave me alone!"

I am hysterical. I just want this to be over. Why can't I just be left alone? I put my attention on the road quickly -- I am being diverted to a detour. As we stop, a vision of a horrific car accident beams into my mind. I see the person driving and it's ME!

I cry out, "You will not take me!"

Horrified, I push away the thought. I am so tired. The pain is immense and I'm already doing all I can to push it away. I think there's no way it can get worse. Wrong. It intensifies.

I scream, "I hate this! I can't do this, I'm too tired to fight."

Then I begin to feel love and peace emerging around me and coldness in my body. I recognize the feeling, it's Anthony. He is here beside me now, working to fight the darkness, elevate my frequency, and relax.

Breathe through the pain. It's one of the relaxation techniques I have begun to do. With Anthony's help I begin to come back to center and relax. The feeling of his presence surrounds me.

I pull into the parking lot at work and hear him say, Talk to Roz, she can help you.

My workday begins with me alone in the office. I feel more centered, enough to begin my spiritual protection and morning spiritual practice. When my vibratory frequency is low, my work schedule is quieter. My angels and guides protect my energy from being further zapped.

I ask Anthony to come into my body again and help remove some of this heaviness sitting on my chest like iron weights. There is so much pain, it makes my heart physically hurt. He tells me it's an effect of the heaviness of grief. His energy enters my body as I have requested. He fills my heart space with white light. I begin to weep, then my whole body vibrates and becomes freezing cold.

Me: Anthony please help me.

Anthony: *Understand, Ma, I can only do so much -- I cannot intervene in your life lesson. You must learn and grow through this. Fight your way through the darkness to get to the light. You are tired but you must not quit. I am your beacon of light through the darkness. Follow me, Ma. Let me help you.*

Me: I am so depleted, I just want to leave here. This life is too hard for me now.

Anthony: *Ma, don't even say that out loud!! Your words have power. You know this. I am frustrated that you are making this much harder than it should be. You understand where I am and that I am happy, this should be enough for you. What don't you understand about this? I'm right here with you.*

Me: You don't understand what it is like to be left behind, to be here and to suffer without you. In spirit form, you are happy living your life as it is now, doing your soul's work. But here, it's not just me and my fatigue; the dark is relentless. I'm fighting with all I got but some days I just can't. I thought that I could fight them off but I can't.

Anthony: *Ma, you can do this. You must do another past life regression, there is more I need you to see. It will help you to understand clearly why we have contracted this lesson in this life.*

Me: I will try, I am just so tired. I am not sleeping well again and I am just tired. I just do not want to do this.

Anthony: *There is no try, Ma.*

I can sense his frustration with me. Anthony has pushed me periodically but never did I feel frustration from him as I do now. If spirit could feel anything negative, this would be it. Where they are there is no negativity. No ill feelings, regret, or anger.

Anthony: *Ma, up until now you have sacrificed your entire existence. It is time for you to relinquish control, trust me, and trust what I tell you. I am here to guide you. There is much riding on this.*

I feel his presence begin to leave and a higher frequency vibration fills my energy field. That's better! I put on some uplifting tones and do energy healing on myself. I finally begin to feel more like myself.

Roz comes into the office and I tell her what has been happening with me. I share with her that it seems like the annoying games of the dark things are minimal in my home -- there's so much organite protecting that space. But I am being attacked in the car, and my family is being attacked outside the areas of protection. I am questioning my own visions. I ask Roz, "Do you think I am going to get into an accident?"

Rozlyn Reynolds, an amazing psychic, has been doing this work for more than 30 years. I value her friendship and trust her with my life and my family's life. She tells me: "They are using your power to get you to manifest the accident. If you'd affirmed at that moment that you accept the vision of the accident, it would have happened -- and you would have manifested it. You were wise to push it away, out of your mind, and deny it. You must get more organite in the car and to wear. Dark entities are very cunning. This should help you. Take back your power."

We collect the organite and put it in my car. Now, I add spiritual protection and always surround myself in the light whenever I get in the car. As I am immersed in the light I call in Archangel Michael and St. Christopher.

I'm feeling much better, but more help is needed. Much more.

Calling in Reinforcements

It is time to go see Sedonah.

She reached out to me and we made an appointment to have a session, and boy do I need it. Sedonah is a beautiful and powerful healer who uses sound and energy. I explain to her that Anthony is here and has been in contact with me. He is very adamant about me following his guidance and doing the inner work I need to do.

Our session begins and immediately I see Anthony in the room; he is sewing together a red heart that has been broken down the middle. Sedonah senses him as well.

He remains with us to guide Sedonah through the healing with me, working through her, moving her hands where needed, directing her to which instruments to use. He asks Sedonah to do another session in a few weeks -- the healing would take time to integrate. She agrees.

That session was life-altering, as you'll see later.

That evening I leave for home and don't cry all the way home in the car -- a change from the "normal" routine. I have to keep my frequency up to protect my family from the malevolent beings, and I'm charged up from my session with Sedonah. I take a salt bath and try to relax for the remainder of the evening. To raise the frequency in the house I play uplifting music, burn sage and light candles. I set the tone by doing some chanting. I am feeling pretty focused when I hear:

You can run, but you can't hide.

By nature I am a warrior, a fighter. That warrior runs through my blood. I shoot back at the dark voice, "You underestimate me! Do not forget who you are fucking with. You will not take me without a fight -- and trust me, it is not a fight you want to undertake. I am a warrior!"

They slink away, their presence gone.

As I get ready for bed I feel Anthony's presence. I light my candle and say my prayers for the evening. I thank all that surrounded me on this day. I see a doorway begin to open in my room. In through the doorway walks Anthony at the forefront of a V formation with many angels and guides. I am overwhelmed and begin to weep. The feeling of love embraces me like a warm blanket comforting me all day long. It is hard to even put into words the feeling of love that encompasses my entire being.

Anthony declares:

Ma, these angels, and beings are here to help you. I need you to keep your frequency as high as possible now. It is imperative. I will be bringing in many more helpers as we move through this deep expansion in your world at this time. Shine the white light directly into the face of fear -- it is of the utmost importance for you to continue to follow this path. This time of expansion is quite necessary. You begin to see it unfold.

Untold truths,

dark will crumble,

be there, shining the light as a beacon for all to see.

The dark is fighting with a vengeance against being brought into the light. They cannot hide their malevolent nature; it will be front and center for all to see. Many are under dark attacks at the moment; surround your world in light and shine some planetary healing energy out in your realm.

The angels begin to fade away as I am once again assured that my beautiful son is here, supporting me always. He will ensure that I have the necessary information as well as the tools to carry forth my duties to fulfill this mission.

As I begin to fall asleep, I see words being sent to me, chapters for the next book. I fall into a deep slumber knowing I am forever cradled in the light. Guided by this amazing light-being that I call my son Anthony Joseph "Butters" in this lifetime, and have called other beloved names in other lifetimes. I feel truly blessed that he chose me to be his mother.

This book is really his book.

I JUST WANT TO HAVE A VOICE TO

HELP PEOPLE HEAL

I just want to have a voice people will heal from. That is all.

-Anthony Joseph, 2016

Anthony's voice continues to push me to do the work of healing while writing his book. The information coming through from him is extensive, describing where this part of our journey together is headed as we move forward together. We are creating a new understanding not only of the spirit world but the intricate connection that carries on between us as we use these words to help others learn there is no death. The information flowing through is a way for others to understand that we are not alone after a loved one sheds their physical body, but rather they are still beside us, guiding through the healing process.

Pain can be a driving force for you to make changes necessary for your life. Grief can also catalyze that change. How we behave correlates directly with what goes on in our thoughts. If we are consumed by grief from the loss of a loved one, our thoughts can be full of agonizing pain. Our brain can be in a state of fear, making it much more overactive while grieving.

By understanding that the process of grief is just as important as verbalizing how the grief is making you feel, you can begin to understand that you hold the power in the process of your healing. I can focus on Anthony being gone in body and on how much I miss him, or I can focus on him being very much alive and present in personality and spirit. You can too, and you don't need to have psychic abilities to do it.

Writing helps me get my feelings out onto paper, releasing some of the heaviness. Grief can make you feel numb, depressed, and foggy. It is difficult to come to an understanding that your loved one was such an intricate part of your existence and now they are no longer here in the physical.

It is quite an adjustment, but it is my belief that you must feel it to heal it. And that can be a jagged pill to swallow. With the help of your loved one in spirit you can begin recognizing there is a new way to heal from grief. Throughout this book I am sharing not only energy healing experiences, but ways spirit communicates with us to help us. Our loved ones continue on beside us, reminding us they are still here. Not gone. Here.

Helping others has been a passion of mine since I can remember. I was always on the side of the underdog, wanting to help those who were down on their luck. My son also wanted to help people heal with his words while he was here and from where he is now. His feelings about being an empath are found throughout his writings. When he was with us he shared his messages through writing but also loved speaking publicly. He would talk to anyone, anywhere at any time. His destiny was agreed on long before he incarnated as Anthony; he would fulfill his purpose in helping others while here on Earth, and after he shed his body.

The Witching Hour

I met with him again this morning in the wee hours, 3:33 a.m. "The witching hour" as we in the business call it. The veil is very thin at this time and it is easier for spirit to communicate with us. Anthony, however, communicates all day, every day, with me. When I need him he is there, sometimes just observing, sometimes checking in, and other times interacting with everyone in our circle.

I ask him to explain to me how we are going to use his voice through me to help people heal from loss.

Ma, you are starting to see the bigger picture, us together at this time when your planet is ascending quickly. We are going to write together and teach others about grief, loss, and connection with spirit. How to learn to process these feelings. A complete program of healing. This could not have been accomplished had I not left. Remember the contract, this was all scripted. Do not forget that.

When this book comes out it will show others that everyone has the ability to communicate with spirit in one way or another. Just because a loved one leaves the physical doesn't mean your relationship ceases to exist. It is stronger than ever. When we understand this process it is easier for us to grasp the truth that there is no death, we are still connected, and you can get your answers directly from your loved ones in spirit.

Learn that everyone has this innate ability to communicate with spirit and we can change the way we look at death. There is no death. We are all spirit living a physical existence and therefore have the divine right to connect with it. Our voices together shall help others understand that grief is a necessary part of what we have contracted as the growth process for our soul.

Aside from that I want to help you explore further the path of grief. I can feel the heaviness in your heart. I know there are days when you are overwhelmed. I get frustrated that you are moving along well one moment and the next you are frozen in grief. I am trying to help you move through that pain but will not be able to remove it all. There is work that you have to do to help to move it. Also, solicit the help of others on your path. They are able to help you when it gets too much for you.

"Anthony, I want to understand. Please tell me more."

Unbeknownst to me at the time when I was in your world, I was already subconsciously aware of who I was but could not understand. I longed for a place that I knew was home, but never felt that I could find it. I was at a place in the last few years where I was at my happiest. I had gotten my shit together and was beginning to understand clearly my path. I started writing my book, but rarely did I believe I was capable of bringing it to reality.

My book was going to help people heal through my words, my experiences.

I never felt quite here or there when I was on Earth, and when I left I did not understand what was to come, but I had a re-membrance; I have always written from my heart and wanted so much to write the book of my dreams, to help others with my voice. I now know that it was all in the divine timing of what was to be. This longing I had inside would come to fruition, just not in the way that I thought it would at the time. I do not have any regrets or remorse. I am glad that I am still carrying out my purpose on the other side of the veil.

Don't you see, Ma, it is you and me together now taking it to the next level. We are writing this book together, and my voice will help others heal, that's all I ever wanted.

What a profound effect all of it will make on the planet. It is not only about us. It's about the evolution of the people on Earth, teaching them about the connection [with spirit]. Not to fear it, and to embrace the divine gift each of us is given.

Knowing we never are truly ever alone. Never have been and never will be.

I see you are thinking.

(Telepathic communication is amazing; he knows what I am thinking before I think it.)

So how do we take it from here to there?

Very easy, follow the guidance I am laying out for you. It's the trail to the opening in the field that will bring you to a never-before known level of existence. Having this constant connection with me requires you to make some deep changes within. I learned a great deal while I was in Earth school, and those lessons carry with me in the afterlife. I am using them to further my growth here, as well as further your growth.

Healing is taken for granted in your culture. People want an easy fix to problems. Following the advice of others, they are always looking outside of themselves for the answers, when inside the answers shall remain. It is when the ego gets involved that we can no longer see our true connection to self.

I also continue to heal while I am here. There were Earthly things that my soul needed to heal from. When we arrive in the next life it's like a shower blanketing us in warmth, similar to what I do when I enter your body for healing.

Healing is first and foremost, but you know this.

After all, isn't that what it is all about? Helping others understand and grow. To heal.

I begin to feel Anthony's presence leaving. Then I come back to center in my body and look at the clock. It's 5:15. The sun hasn't shown its face. I was with him for a long time. I lay down to recover from the session. It takes an immense amount of energy to bridge the gap with him for such a long time, and to feel the feelings I am feeling, and to translate everything into words.

Our sessions bring me closer to him. I don't feel as lost as I do at other times. There are still times I am in sheer disbelief of everything that has occurred in such a short time -- not even half a year ago Anthony walked among us.

Where is this all going? I am just hanging on for the ride. Anthony says together we will bring our voice to the forefront of healing. I understand now what Anthony says about healing and how things need to change in our world. There is much we still need to learn through the process of healing. Healing in all senses of the word, as well as healing grief.

Throughout the day I spend much time busy just living life, but still with a feeling that there is more to talk about with Anthony. The day comes and goes and I get sidetracked. Before I know it I'm ready for bed. I promise him that in the morning I will connect with him.

The following morning I begin my spiritual practice and immediately Anthony's presence enters my meditation. I can feel his presence begin to engulf my field, instantly filling me with love and peace.

Of course, I still cry, I am still grieving and healing.

He comes to stand beside me. His presence overflows from him to me, expanding his energy out to me. I begin to shiver -- cold, so cold.

Ma, your body is equipped with all you need for healing to occur. There is never a separation -- not in body nor spirit. We are one and always will be one. Forged within a soul are codes of light to activate all you need for healing, you just need to ask to access them. Our bodies were designed to allow perfect guidance from your higher self while in human form. You can fulfill your destiny to heal if you so choose to do that. I have been given instructions for you to follow to download the codes of intricate awareness and understanding encoded within your DNA, allowing deeper access to your human genome. Spend more time in nature and meditation, and take time to rest as you upgrade your being.

Boyton Canyon is waiting for you. There, you will download new information to use to advance your understanding and ability. There are new upgrades and codes to be downloaded into your being. A new upgraded system to help anchor in the changes that you have seen with your new modality.

I am bringing in a world-renowned physicist, Sydney Brenner (Nobel laureate, 2002) to help us understand all there is to know about DNA. Mapping DNA like this has never been explained in human form. Great knowledge is coming to your people. DNA can be manipulated merely by understanding it can be manipulated. Visualization is quite important here, as well as physically working the rungs of the DNA with your mental hands -- you will be a psychic surgeon, Ma! The power will work through you to remove diseased areas and replace rungs of the DNA ladder with new, improved crystalline rungs

As we go forward there will be a self-mastery that comes from working the DNA. Expect mistakes, they are part of the learning process. Do not worry; you will get there. Every good student must make mistakes when they are forging new territory. This information is for the increased ability to put the power of the people back in their own hands.

The first book [this book] will provide a mere snippet of information to come through to begin the learning. The next books will go into full detail of the process and how it is to be worked. It will involve the process of shifting from pain to peace, too.

Remember, you are breaking new ground as you step into the new awareness of this level of healing. I am helping you amplify your healing not only on yourself but on others. Please call me into your sessions and watch the beauty that arises as we begin to work more closely together.

There is no time better than the present to forge this new ground. You have many questions, I know, but one day at a time, Ma. You are my flower and I am your bee as we pollinate the new energy codes to you. Rest! You must take enough time to rest to assimilate the changes that are occurring quite rapidly. Bring that light in you, everything you have in you, to fight the dark entities. They want you taken out, and it is up to us to make sure that doesn't happen.

Remember not only you but Sophia: she is next in the lineage. Train her in the arena as I am training you. She will also be unlocking further codes at the perfect times as she ages. We are in this together, Ma. All of us.

I'm out,

Ant.

As my son leaves, I feel peaceful and interested to know more, astounded by this new information that he has shared with me. I search the internet for Dr. Brenner. Lo and behold, up pops biographical information about Sydney Brenner. Dr. Brenner passed away in April 2019, and he is now working together with my son. He is a giant in the field of molecular biology, and he made seminal contributions to the scientific understanding of DNA.

Whoa!

I am in awe of the information coming through, not only from Anthony but from my inner guidance, angels, and spirit guides. Oftentimes it comes to me completely out of the blue, followed by confirmation of its validity and truth.

There is so much for us to learn from the spirit world. A guide, my son, is directing me where I need to go. He shows me what needs to be done and I do it. There are days he blows me away with the messages he shares. It keeps me going. I couldn't do it alone, and never should I fear ever being alone.

That night sleep comes on quickly, and I go into my dreams knowing that divine guidance and protection are with me. And to think that dark things and dread filled my dreams just a short time ago. Now I am surrounded by the army of heaven. We've come a long way so quickly.

EXPANSION: GROWING BEYOND

LIMITS

It can be difficult for some people to step outside their comfort zone -- for me that is definitely the case. Who doesn't like their comfort? But nothing beautiful ever grows in these surroundings.

Awakening to see and understand new things doesn't always make sense at first, but there is a subconscious knowing. Grasping the vastness of the world we live in comes by receiving information through many channels. Through books, television shows, online videos, and music. Through meditation, dreams, and exercise. Through uplifting creativity and devastating loss. Through conversations and whispered questions between friends about subjects that are normally off-limits.

The old paradigm that the world is just a big machine, and the human being is just a biological meat puppet, is a lie. Despite desperate efforts by the protectors of that orthodoxy to conceal the truth, there are too many channels. The truth is leaking out and spreading person to person. And best of all, it's the truth you already know inside you because it is imprinted in the roots of your being. Once that bell is rung, it continues vibrating within you, and the resonance spreads out all directions to attract to you, information, knowledge, people, and experience so you too can live in the light. You can know the truth. You can be the truth.

There is more to know than we have been taught. It's like finding a secret room in your home -- the door opens and of course, you want to know what's inside. But will you muster the courage to step over that threshold? It's dark in there at first, and what you encounter will make you uncomfortable. It will challenge your beliefs and crack you open so the light can penetrate into your depths.

Fortunately, people want to understand everything they are experiencing, and it is pushing them out of their comfort zone. Many of my clients have come searching for answers. They are beginning to hear, see, feel and experience things for the first time, and encountering the truth in ways they can't deny. Their comfort zone is no longer comfortable. It is all happening at a time that we believe is a turning point for our world.

People are awakening.

We are ascending.

Wake Up!

This morning I woke up to someone hitting my bed -- an out-and-out slam! It made me jump like a scared cat. But wait, I'm the only one home. "What the hell!" I mutter. Then I sense Anthony is here and ask, was that you?

I am here for our morning chat, Ma.

"Whoa, what a way to wake someone up!"

I collect my senses and ask him to explain what it is like at that moment where he is right now.

It is sort of surreal. Unknown memories flood in from other lives, future lives. It takes me to a place of unknown love. A time capsule of sorts of my lifetimes on Earth and in other dimensions.

My oversoul speaks to me often.

My main guide is here with me showing me the way, but I am also left to have time on my own. This guide has been with me from the beginning. You know him as Grandpa Benny. He keeps me aligned with what I need to do for you and others. A regimented plan. I can meet with others who are on this side of the veil, as well as meet with you guys on Earth. I enjoy floating back and forth.

I also enjoy learning to play with all the energy that I am. It is so interesting to me to be able to float between these worlds and do the things I'm learning to do. I'm learning to shift into physical form in pictures, as well as leave a physical imprint of my energy for you to see. I will be bringing in more physical "proof" that we -- the so-called "deceased" -- are still here.

I am often guided on this journey. And I am at peace. Love and peace filters through me -- not only something that fills me, but that I AM. Two phases of existence.

I see you often. Sometimes I just come in and observe. Knowing you need me, I pop in. Most times you are aware, other times you are too deep in grief. So I just sit with you.

I am happy, and I am without human pain. But I do feel your pain to an extent. It saddens me when you are hurting so much, but I am here to help you.

We will be meeting three times a week, and I will be integrating my energy with yours as you learn what it is like to house all this light energy in a human body. There is no way for me to truly show you how I feel unless I enter your body. It can be a lot to handle, but I know you can do this. I will take it slow and amp up the energy when needed. I want you to record the sessions and begin documenting weekly assignments as we work together so that you can go back and look at all this when the time is right.

You taught me profound lessons, and now it is my turn to teach you. As you follow my lead, the beauty of 'what is' will lighten your load.

The beauty here is way beyond any beauty I have ever known.

I know this is all still a shock to your system. I am with you always. Please know that. There are many others with me here. Some you know and others you never knew. There is so much I am learning as I grow and expand through this dimension.

In the place where I am, we congregate. It is my Eden -- our Eden. Perfect and beautiful beyond words to describe. You have been here during our sessions, but your physical body is acting like a dampener to limit the experience. Soon you will transcend those limits and merge with the light. In this place we congregate to discuss how to put into human words the things we know simply as reality and truth. There really are no words to describe, but we do our best.

The music here is beautiful, too. The frequencies are amazing. I am wrapped in a blanket of soothing peace. The sunshine is bright and beautiful, filling and expanding me.

Helping you helps me at the same time. It will do the same for you when we connect. Then afterwards go sit in the sun and anchor in the energy.

I am not far off in some distant galaxy. I am right here with you. Always! You feel my energy when I come in. We are learning together what is to come of this union. By far, the most beauty will come with what we show to others on our path. There are no coincidences; this time is right for us to do this work together. There is no other way that it would have worked.

I ask, what else can you tell me about the expansion?

You are doing great, easy-peasy. I am sure that you don't think so. As you will see, as you expand more with the light when I enter your body, the pain shall dissipate into a mere memory. Allow me to continue guiding you through this process.

Expansion is occurring rapidly. You expand so you can incorporate more energy and more light and do more with it -- it is the nature of consciousness to expand and assimilate, and that builds inner authority and ability to control. It is like a kingdom expanding to encompass more and exert its influence farther out. And in the center of that kingdom, the heart of that domain is your soul. By going deep within yourself, you create a counter-movement that simultaneously expands outward. Think of it like a drop of water landing on a calm pool. The wave spreads outward but also collapses inward.

You need to make sure you rest. I cannot stress enough the importance of rest for you. I will continue to send you to the people who need you and the people you need.

Keep on writing the book, the first of many for you. Do not become overwhelmed. You will see how easily it will all flow from you as you move forward with this expansion. You will be teaching others, but first you need to fully know and experience it.

I am asking you to start to run. The words will come easier without the heaviness presently in your body. Aerobic activity is helpful in moving some of the heavy energy sitting in your chest. The light energy from me will help with this, too.

I love you to the end of time and again, Ma. No doubts, just fierce, badass energy flowing free from my heart to yours. Growth and expansion, here and now. Surrender to the infinite without feeling the need to control it all. You have so much to offer the world with your light. This light is growing and ever-expanding. Me through you, Ma.

I'm out,

Ant.

He's out, and I am wiped out. Growth, expansion, grief -- only rest and downtime will help me assimilate the changes. I know what he is talking about. He entered my body before as he brought me to peace from the brink of darkness, and those times were only hints of what is to come when his spirit can enter further into me.

I lose track of time when I am with him. I truly want to spend all my time in the higher realms just to be with him. These realms are so beautiful and nothing like I have ever experienced before. Without the light I would not be here writing this today. My son helped to save me from the darkness that crept in after he died.

Expanding rapidly. Processing grief and fighting the dark. ...I guess I need to add Superwoman to my repertoire.

The Gateway to Infinity

As I begin to go through my day I feel him everywhere with me. He is ever-present in my home. I am blanketed in a field of peace. It feels good to be expanding and having my son with me in spirit guiding me. He does not seem as far away as he did in the beginning. Maybe because I am working through the grief rather than let it encompass my entire being. I allow myself to have the time to meditate, exercise, rest. All of this work takes a toll on the physical body. I know I must rest or I will get sick.

I am tired so I decide to rest, following his guidance and my inner guidance. We spend so much time running rapidly through life we forget how important it is to have balance. I lay down and it is not long before a field of energy opens up near the doorway to my bedroom, close to the ceiling.

"Ant, is that you?"

Yep, you got it, Ma.

He cautions, *I know when you sleep you want to leave your body behind. You can visit here but you cannot stay. You can move through the elevator of consciousness and meet me across the gateway, I will be there waiting for you.*

"OK," I say and begin to fall asleep.

I drift off but my mind stays awake in a hypnagogic state of consciousness (between asleep and awake, a state in which I can clearly see spirit in every form). I enter the gateway. There's Anthony dressed in white linen, his hair flowing freely. He looks so happy and peaceful. He glows. Light radiates outwards from him that I have not seen to this extent previously from him. It is breathtaking. Speechless, I sit for a moment and take in the brightness of this beautiful platinum light that surrounds him. I do not cry but I want to; I am surrounded by peace and love once again.

"What is this glow about you?"

The brighter you shine, the brighter I shine. The expansion that we spoke about not only pertains to you but it pertains to me as well. I know you do not understand where all this is going yet but I do. There is so much more for you to know.

...Expansion.

I have seen the blueprint of the future, and soon your understanding will deepen. I know you are in pain, the heaviness is weighing on your heart. I am cuddling you in light and trying to alleviate some of the heaviness. You see, Mom, up here we have our work to do, too.

The beauty that will arise from this pain will help so many. You will grow amazing and beautiful things from this broken heart. It is an intricate puzzle that sits before you, can you see it? Or maybe you cannot yet. But it's there. We planned all of this -- it's the bigger picture.

I am supporting you as you grow through this expansion. Time does not heal all wounds; healing is what heals all wounds. It is not linear; there is no set pattern to grief. It is a process as intricate as your fingerprint. It must be tailored to each individual's needs and at their own pace.

I see your neurons that need reconnecting to expand your brain capacity. This expansion is also occurring within you on a physical level. We are doing this work together, Ma, as we grow together. You will begin to use more of your brain, and this will help the neurons. It is time to see Sedonah again for some healing. She will help you further connect these neurons with her sound healing. I see the explosion of neurons reactivating. It will lead to remembering who you really are.

Right on cue, my cell phone buzzes with a text message. It's from Sedonah, reaching out to me to offer another healing session. Synchronicity is a regular feature of my life now -- everything comes to me as it's needed -- and I'm learning to go with the flow. My perception is changing, too, and the processes of learning and growth are accelerating.

I will expand greatly over the next few weeks -- it is life-changing -- and it is exhilarating but exhausting. Lots of rest is needed to integrate it. Anthony insists, and Sedonah is a member of this magic circle coming together around Anthony's guidance -- of course I will accept her offer to have another healing session!

It's quite different than the last one. Last time, she focused on my heart. This time she focuses on my head. My scalp tingles and that feeling comes on again; Anthony enters the session to observe and interact with us. Color and light explode in my mind's eye. Neurons reconnect energetically, just like Anthony said would happen. I see past lives emerge right before me, giving me a clearer understanding of who I am at a soul level.

This is the turning point where a new life opens up. I am born again. Sedonah's sound magic absorbs into my being and penetrates my cells. The rapid changes occurring integrate and become a permanent part of me. I am synthesizing spirit into my body. I breathe in deeply knowing I am again divinely guided and protected by my son.

After the session, Sedonah shares her version of the experience and says it is like nothing she has ever seen before. "This reconnection will help you exponentially expand, Terri-Ann!"

As I expand, Anthony expands. How does one explain expansion? Is it felt? Understood? How do we go beyond what we know?

Spirit creates a way for us to see a new world. A quiet world. A world of infinite stillness where quiet opens us up to all that is. Source. Creation. Connection with our ancestors and multidimensional beings that bring knowledge and awakening to our human being. They are there to help us along our path that can at times seem lonely and inundating. We expand to assimilate and control these experiences and the energy that comes with them.

In quiet, limitations are lifted.

Stillness is the thread that binds everything together. When you see behind the curtain that separates physical reality from infinity, what you find is timeless stillness. And in that stillness, that eternal peace, everything is perfect as it is. It's beautiful. As we expand we incorporate more of that perfection, that peace, and that beauty. We begin as a rough lump of clay and the end result, after expansion, is a masterpiece. And we all get there eventually, following our individual paths and going about it our individual ways. We have eternity to make it.

Meditation is a wonderful way to connect with the higher self as well as divine love. When spirits work with us they are helping us open to what is and to all that we are. We have to find the quiet and stillness in meditation to hear them.

It can be difficult for people to listen to their inner knowing. The ego is loud at times. It is important to tune out all the noise to hear spirit.

Many signs come through dreams. It is the easiest way for spirit to communicate with us. During dream time we are free of logic and the egoic mind. Dreams can be very metaphorical and open us up to our potential, showing us what we truly are as spiritual beings temporarily residing in human bodies. We can use the metaphors and symbols offered by our dreams to decipher their messages and find our individual path to expansion.

Dr. Carl Jung, the famous dream psychologist, calls the process "individuation." It means becoming a complete, self-actualized being, and it is a process of expanding to consciously integrate your unconscious and actualize your potential. Your awareness expands outward by going within yourself, and you go within yourself by shutting the hell up for a while and just listening to the stillness within you.

Dream symbols are layered with meaning. Brush away the surface meaning and you find another layer beneath it, then another, then another. Body, mind, heart, spirit -- one dream symbol can speak simultaneously to all layers. Dream symbols are amazingly potent and loaded with information. They not only come from the deeper reality of stillness and peace that underlies what we know as reality, but they are also gateways to it.

Working with dreams is our best way to expand and individuate.

In our dreams we rest and heal. It's the dreaming mind's first priority -- the body must recuperate and rejuvenate. At other times while dreaming we travel in spirit, receive messages, and gather together as a spiritual community in a dimensional space outside of ordinary space-time. These dream experiences are seldom remembered consciously because they occur during the Delta stage of sleep when brainwave patterns are slowest and the conscious mind is totally zonked out. But subconsciously you carry with you everything you learn and experience.

A lot of people are opening, awakening, and beginning to see, hear, and feel messages coming through from the other side. It happens while dreaming and meditating, and at other times.

When you are opening to messages and intuition it is important to remember that expansion occurs in layers as well. It takes time and is not an overnight process. Each human being has their own spiritual path to follow. Free will also plays a role. Spiritual paths challenge us and offer lessons to learn while we are here. This all helps to ensure you are well on your way to opening to the vast processes of awakening and expansion.

I ask Anthony, "what else can you tell me about this expansion?"

Ma, expansion for you is a process of undoing. This undoing is to the thousands of years of cellular memory that have been stored in your DNA and fills you with limiting beliefs.

While not everyone will open to this expansion, to ensure that you are opening to it you shall spend much time in nature and meditation. Quieting the mind to stillness allows for much information to come through to you. While following this guidance it is important to keep track of all that is coming through; it is a puzzle for you to follow.

I am in a process of expansion myself. Here we also undergo changes. I am growing my energy rapidly -- much growth in a short time. Ascending quickly, you could say. I am changing, and growing my energy to expand outwards greatly.

"I have noticed."

This meeting, Anthony has expanded greatly. I see a huge vision of him adorned in white and gold colors. The most breathtaking colors you have ever seen. A gold glow fills his aura. He has up leveled-up.

There are many different levels in the spirit world and I have only seen a few with Anthony since he shed his physical body. I am learning as I go from my greatest teacher. I lost my son and gained the strongest guide.

I'm glad I didn't know what I agreed to in our soul contract when all this happened. I would have dialed up God and demanded, who do you think you are taking my son from me? No way would I have agreed to it, but now that I see the beauty growing from it, I can't argue (as much). I see the higher purpose at work here.

Pain, grief, darkness, despair -- they are flames that burn away everything that weighs down spirit. This path is one of constant challenge. Comfort? Say goodbye and trade it for the peace that surpasses understanding.

NEAR DEATH AND OUT OF BODY

EXPERIENCES, PREMONITIONS,

DREAMS

I n Anthony's journal he recounts a dream that involves him visiting the other side. He didn't know the nature of his dream at the time in 2016, but looking back now I know what it was.

He begins, "In my dream, I approach a set of huge mahogany doors and sense on the other side are paths leading to other lives I've lived. One door has a warning sign on it. It's the door I'm most drawn to. I'm curious. The door opens on its own, and suddenly my vision narrows like I'm in a tunnel.

"I step through the doorway and move forward. Three hallways are before me, each leading to different areas. Serenity fills me. And love. Immense love so strong and deep words can't describe it. It is a love like no other. The beauty surrounding me blows me away.

"I float to a hallway I am drawn to, not really understanding how I'm going to get there. I see a large gleaming structure sitting on a cloud formation as if in suspended animation. There are windows made of orange and red glass with green filaments mixed in. It feels peaceful, yet there is some fear inside me. Fear of the unknown, but there's a familiarity to it. A spiral of light surrounds me with love. It feels like I am home.

"I am alone, yet at the same time I am not. Then the scene shifts and I am floating away. The love surrounding me is so strong and so, so brilliant -- like nothing like I have ever experienced."

Anthony asked me for my thoughts about his dream soon after he had it. I felt the deep impact it had on him. I tell him it could mean a lot of things but intuitively I feel he is seeing what it's like to experience existence from the other side while still here in the body. It's a taste of the afterlife.

The conversation then progresses to talking about death. Emphatically he tells me, "Death is merely a doorway to another dimension. This doorway will lead you home and you will be reunited with your family. I am not scared; I know what lies ahead."

The dream gave him a new understanding of life, and he vowed to begin life anew. He was drawn to read the book *Infinite Jest* by David Foster Wallace, and around this time one of his friends from high school committed suicide. These events gave Anthony a new perspective.

The realization that we are here in this body for a limited time to learn what we need to learn has immense power. I understood this at the time but failed to realize that Anthony's dream prepared him for his physical death by letting him experience what comes next and feel the love through the fear. Three years later he would leave his physical body behind for good.

Like Mother, Like Son

Premonitions. Out of body journeys. I've had my share.

These experiences are awakenings for the people who have them, giving them the undeniably personal knowledge that life is much grander than we think it is. A premonition that comes true or an experience out of the body cracks us open and lets us know without a doubt there's so much more to know and experience. It lifts us above the limiting beliefs and indoctrination that form a cage around the limitless spirit. With courage and curiosity we step out of the box and know the truth that life is infinite, and life in a physical body is only the tip of the arrow.

In 2017 my life shifted drastically, a pivotal point that led to a huge spiritual awakening. I was very sick with an upper respiratory infection for almost three weeks. I had a premonition one night of going into cardiac arrest. It scared me shitless. I told my husband it was going to occur in two weeks and he needed to keep a close eye on me. He sort of laughed and shrugged it off, but I knew deep down that it was going to occur. My premonition painted the scene for me vividly.

A few weeks go by and I am still deathly ill with the infection and can't breathe. My airways are constricting. The benadryl I was taking barely worked, and my husband remembered our daughter had some Albuterol left from when she was sick. The dosage he loaded in the nebulizer was tiny. I put on the mask and suck as much of it into my lungs as I can manage.

Ten minutes later I'm gasping for air and clutching my chest. My heart pounds. My body shakes uncontrollably. Realizing the premonition is coming true and I am near death, I manage to motion for him to call 911 before collapsing on the bed.

Everything is happening exactly as I saw in my premonition a few weeks earlier. My spirit lifts out of my body and I hover over the scene and witness it like watching a movie. But unlike my premonition, I float further and further away. I see my family and their pain and tears, and the paramedics working on me, same as my premonition but it's more distant. I'm drifting away.

A feeling of supreme peace washes over me. I just died, but I feel calm and in awe of the amazingly beautiful colors that surround me. My bags are packed, the plane is taxiing. A wonderful new existence awaits me, and despite what's happening with my loved ones back in Earth school, I'm ready to go. They will be OK, and I'm more than OK. I'm eager for what comes next.

Then I hear, "GO BACK!!!"

Instantaneously I begin floating back down to Earth, and the next thing I remember is I'm back in my deathly sick body and being loaded into an ambulance.

The moment is embedded in my brain to this day and will continue to be for the rest of my life, I expect. People who have near death experiences (NDEs) use words such as "profound" to describe it and the lasting impact it has. But the reality is, multiply "profound" by a thousand and it still falls short. Before my NDE I understood there is a place where the spirit travels to after it leaves the body, but experiencing immersion in the loving light is soul-deep knowing. You know what to expect when the time comes to leave Earth, and you know it is wonderful. Returning to typical everyday reality is a letdown.

To some people that statement might sound uncaring, but that perception is based on lack of knowing there's a source of love in this universe that cares for us all and makes everything -- even death -- all right.

Think of death as waking up from a dream. You might feel some attachment to the world you leave behind, but soon it fades in importance because you are back in "reality." Afterlife is the true reality.

My NDE tops the "profound" scale, but it's only one of the myriad personal experiences. They began as premonitions I had as a young child. Thinking at the time I was making these things happen rather than seeing into the future, I turned it off. That reaction is common for children who have no frame of reference for understanding their unusual experiences and no support system for processing them. Turn it off, make it go away.

Now as an adult I know other dimensions exist. I astral travel in my sleep and spend much of my waking time in other dimensions. For me, being on Earth is hard. I need a reprieve at times. I love spending time in other realms with Anthony and otherworldly beings. I've been doing it my entire life, beginning long before I possessed the words and concepts to describe it.

Intense nightmares and frequent astral travel were features of my spiritual reawakening. Astral travel is when the soul separates from the body and can travel to other dimensions. I do this often, and it occurred nightly and very memorably when I was deep into my awakening. Yes, it occurs nightly for all of us anyway, but as I said previously it's not usually remembered.

Roz Reynolds, my friend, and psychic mentor taught me to connect a silver cord to my body before journeying out of the body. She advised in response to an intense dream where I had left my body to astral travel and was suddenly and forcibly brought back in. I was shaking and crying and could not understand where I was.

That night in a dream reptilian beings chase me and my daughters. I run and jump from car to car and make it to my husband but he is entranced. I know if I can get to him and touch him that it will break the trance, but a reptilian woman stops me. We flee and suddenly I'm pulled back into my body. Wham! I wake up scared and unaware of where I am.

I then shake and cry for a long time.

Ever since then I always attach a silver cord whenever I travel in the astral plane so I can always come back to my body and remain aware of being one place in my body and in another place in my spirit. No more surprises! And no more reptilians. Whatever stands in my way in the astral -- dreaming or not -- can be overcome

Dreams

Dreams are another way I am learning more in-depth information. At times, dreams can be a place to release some of the heaviness we are experiencing in life and our emotions. Other times, they can serve as premonitions, allowing us to see into the future (known as precognitive dreams). They can also give us a taste of what life is like in spirit, without a physical body.

Our dreams are deeply meaningful. I equate them to a puzzle. Dreams show us pieces of ourselves to put together to develop personally and spiritually. The dreaming mind knows what the puzzle looks like when completed, and it guides us night and day. You don't have to see the big picture the dreaming mind sees; just keep fitting the pieces together as they're given to you..

It is no coincidence that the editor for this book is an expert in dream interpretation. Soon after a mutual acquaintance put us in contact, my cousin gave me a book for Christmas which my editor wrote -- my cousin had no idea. She bought the book [The Dream Interpretation Dictionary by J.M. DeBord] because something about it appealed to her as a gift for me. Some people might say it is a coincidence, nothing more, but my life unfolds this way all the time, and other spiritual seekers and warriors experience it too. Some people call it synchronicity. You might call it freedom because it enables you to live with a focus on spirit and let everything else take care of itself.

The dark things can enter a place in our dream state and instill fear if we let them -- they tried their damndest with me following Anthony's death. But I'm learning that these experiences serve a higher purpose, too. They make us aware of the need for healing. They confront us with our self-limiting beliefs. Before a rocket launches into outer space it must be checked and rechecked for its structural integrity and ability to function while under stress. The human rocket must also go through the same rigors. If you blast off into the spiritual realms before you're ready, it can harm or even destroy you. So first you are tested while on the ground.

I had a few recurring dreams when my boys were young. In one, a police officer comes to the door and I see myself crying and falling to the floor. I never hear what is said, although I know it can't be good. This scene came true the night that Ant died.

Anthony visits me on the monthly anniversary of his passing. To date I have had five dreams about him, each with a message that leaves me breathless. Run together, the dreams are a sequence. They interrelate, and with each new dream the messages and lessons deepen and broaden. The dreams run together to create a road to follow, and I (or you) can walk that road knowing that everything needed to make the journey will be provided.

My first dream about Anthony following his death occurred four weeks afterward -- it's the dream I shared earlier in the book where grief was blocking me from hearing him clearly. It had such a deep meaning. I needed more time to allow myself to work through my grief while not letting it debilitate me.

My next dream occurred four weeks after the first one. Anthony shows up and my bedroom is dark and dismal. I am alone and feeling frightened, which is not normal for me. Dark energy lurks around me, bringing my biggest fears in and shrouding me in darkness. I'm sitting in the corner of the room. A huge dark cloud hovers over me taking my breath away, sucking the life out of me. It is enjoying every moment and growing bigger.

Then I see Anthony trying to reach me, trying to relay a message but too far away to hear. He begins yelling at me, waving his hands. As he does, the fear becomes bigger and begins to swallow me. Anthony yells, "There is evil in the fear! Diminish the fear, diminish the evil! This is you -- you are seeing your fear brought to life -- but you got this, Ma. Fight back!"

I awoke with a new understanding of how the dark things play on my fears and how to respond. I began using releasing techniques nightly to diminish my fears. My biggest fear is my husband and children being hurt, and I needed to change my thinking about that. Releasing those fears put me back in the driver's seat. Since then, dreams where my husband or children are hurt have all but vanished.

Twelve weeks after Anthony's passing he visits me again in a dream. We were traveling in our RV together. He is driving and has to park it in a tight spot and finally succeeds. He parks and jumps out yelling excitedly, "I did it Ma, I did it! Can you believe I did this!"

In our next session together I am curious about the dream and ask him about it. As always I clear my space and ask to connect. I feel his presence immediately and the emotions are over-whelming. He waits for me to compose myself, and we begin our session.

"Anthony, what was my last dream about? You were driving the RV and jumped out after parking it. You were so happy you did it!"

He smiles, glowing. The most beautiful, luminescent light I have ever seen, noticeably more vibrant than the last time I saw him. He says:

Driving used to make me nervous. And the bigger the vehicle, the bigger my nervousness. Being able to park the RV is a met-aphor for the confidence I've gained and the shift I've made.

Ma, I have shifted as you have shifted. We are interconnected. We are doing our work individually, and we are doing our work together. Don't you see THIS IS US. While we step forward into the unknown we are looking at a new horizon of change. There is much to be gained with the knowledge coming through. We might not understand everything at this exact moment as I am still learning as well, but there is much to be gained from our relationship as mother and son.

There will be another shift coming for you as you regain mo-mentum and move forward to the infinite. Still it is necessary for you to keep your frequency as high as possible. I know you have a hard time and the darkness that interferes with you is chipping away at the exterior of your barrier.

It is OK to ask others for help. Reach out to your friends. You have to keep running for exercise, listening to uplifting music, meditating more frequently and resting. This will begin to open you up to the new weekly wisdom that you and I will be sharing together. Watch for it.

I got you, Ma.

Ant.

Gratitude fills me as my son's energy fades. I just miss him so much physically. I have asked him for a hug but have yet to receive one. I am still holding on to hope, of receiving one. I ask again, "Next shift maybe I can get a hug, baby boy?" I weep again. My pain pales in comparison to the feeling of having this amazing connection, but I yearn for more. It is still a big adjustment not having my son in the physical with us.

He visited me again right before the first Thanksgiving following his passing. I shared it on my Facebook business page @ sassysouladvice -- it was so amazing. It has similarities with Anthony's dream that I described at the beginning of this chapter.

My dream: I wake up and a massive dragon comes to me as I watch in amazement. He flies down and puts a beautiful emerald gem in my heart space. It lights up. As if by magic, poof,

Anthony appears right in front of me. He takes my hand. We jump on the dragon and fly to a castle, the most beautiful and majestic castle I have ever seen.

We enter and the castle is full of mahogany doors. Each door contains a message. We look at a few messages, then at this present life and its message -- this life is just one of many. The message is, *I cannot do my work without you and you cannot do your work without me.* Reiterating this message, we are one in the same.

We shared many laughs and tears on this journey in my dream. As we depart and say our goodbyes my son reminds me again:

You are never without me.

As above, so below.

Within you lies me.

Take this emerald gem and keep it in your heart space. Surround it with energy daily to invigorate you.

You are an amazing mom and I couldn't have done what I did without you in this lifetime.

We chose this and many lifetimes before.

It's time for you to drop your baggage and soar like me.

I wake up feeling refreshed and invigorated, smiling, feeling the warmth and amazement of the most beautiful time with my son in a dream visit. Each visit is so profound. I journal the experience while the memories are fresh -- I suggest you do the same by tracking your dream life in a journal. I have never been more sure of where I am headed, and I know Anthony will always guide me.

Right before Christmas 2019 Anthony visited me again in a dream. In it our family gathered for the holiday at my aunt and uncle's house. We settle in to eat dinner when the front door flies open. In walks Anthony wearing jeans and a t-shirt. Everyone is awed -- they are all able to see him there, too -- it isn't just me. I say to him, "How can everyone see you?"

He laughs and says," I am dead but I am still fucking here. Isn't this great!?"

We all laugh. It IS great. And it is so him, his personality. He sits with us and we have a merry time eating and drinking and sharing many stories and hugs.

I know what he meant. Our family is learning slowly through this process that Anthony's presence is powerful and everlasting. I awaken from that dream feeling blessed to have such an amazing son in spirit who can share his existence where he is now, with us still on Earth.

The soul contract I used to hate is now a blessing. Yes, I agreed to this. We agreed. Never have I experienced such darkness. And never has the light returned so brightly and beautifully. He tells me not only did I agree to this but it was my idea. (Can't argue with that.) It was for my soul's growth and I understand that better than ever.

Healing Grief

Grief is not something you have to get over, I am slowly learning. While meditating this morning I hear those words echo in my mind. It's a sign to begin this chapter on grief.

Grief can be all-consuming. It changes over time. And it can be heavy and overwhelming. It takes a toll on your mental, emotional, and physical states. At one time or another we all grieve. Grieving can be brought on by the loss of a loved one, a pet, a relationship, a job.

The grieving process has many facets to it. While everyone is different, I am learning that for me grief is a daily process of undoing the heavy pain that sits in my chest. There is no finish line for grief, no set amount of time for it to run its course. How I grieve is as individual as my fingerprint. My parents and children all grieve differently, each one processing the loss of Anthony in their own way.

Community support can have a great impact on our own healing. It helps to connect with others who have been there and are able to understand. Since Anthony's passing I have found and made many connections with others who have lost children. The experiences are synchronicities -- these encounters are not random. Anthony is guiding me to these people as well.

The impact is huge as you begin to understand the grieving process and heal. The pain might never go away but your perception of it will change as you learn and grow. Grieving is unique for each individual, but for everyone there are many things to do that can help. They might not resonate with you so take what resonates and leave the rest. This is the process that I still use daily to help me make it through.

First and foremost I raise my vibration as soon as I wake up. I play uplifting music. I lay in bed, call in spiritual protection and ask to connect with Anthony. Then I begin to meditate. I ask for knowledge of what my mind, body and soul needs, and I make time to follow the guidance I'm given no matter what it is. If it is rest, I rest. If it is water, I make sure to drink plenty that day. I also incorporate energy healing into my day. It helps to align my energy and bring me to a place of peacefulness.

As I move through my day I allow time for feelings to come up. If it is anger, I allow the anger to flow. As long as it is not overtaking me, I take time to write about it and whatever else comes up. Writing and journaling help me to process and gain personal distance to observe and reflect.

Nothing could have prepared me for what I lived through when Anthony transitioned, but this advice can be a guide to help others along their path. On my darkest days of grief, I cling to life, hoping that the day will end so I can go to bed and get a reprieve. On my best days, I am able to interact with my family and laugh and enjoy the moment. As we are entering the six-month mark since Anthony transitioned, I can say there are more days when I am laughing, but still there are days when grief takes me down to my knees.

Grief is a process that must be worked individually. There are many stages to grief and they don't go in order. You can be in more than one stage at a time and there is no time limit to the stages. You might skip stages and stay in one stage longer than others. There is no normal amount of time to grieve, and everyone experiences their pain differently. The emotions range from severe depression to intense anger and everything in between. You can feel physical pain in your chest and head. It is important to know that what is normal for you might not be normal for someone else.

Energy healing and writing are the two best ways I have learned to work through my grief.

Grief can be a daunting process. I can be moving through my day entirely focused on my work and then out of the blue the lightning strikes: my son is not here, he is dead. I am quickly reminded that he really is here, of course. He shed his physical body, is all. He's not gone.

Driving along in my car today, I am visited by Anthony. He sits in the passenger seat. I can feel him and hear him:

Please begin to allow much time for rest. You take care of everybody but now is the time that you must extend that care to yourself. Do not feel bad for saying no, for taking extra time to rest and taking personal time. You are going to get sick if you do not. I am working to protect your heart. Do more energy healing

*on your heart. Your spirit is tired. It is time to give up the guilt
and put you first.*

Love never ends, Ma.

Times like these make me so grateful to have my son here with
me. Yes, in a different form I can't physically hug and love on,
but right here beside me nonetheless. He knows what I need to
hear and when I need to hear it. His visits are quick sometimes.
He pops in and out and reminds me he is here. He'll remind me
a million times if necessary.

It does help me to have him here with me always. In this way
my process of grief is so different than normal. Two hours after
my son died, he'd already returned, and his presence has never
left me for long.

We are taught that death is the end and whatever comes next,
if anything, can't be known. We are taught to fear what we can't
see and deny everything that can't be proven scientifically.
Not only are these beliefs untrue, but they are also deliberate-
ly imposed on us. Therefore, they are lies. And lies come with
agendas. The agenda is to prevent us from knowing ourselves
as infinite spiritual beings. The agenda is to take our power,
to control us. False beliefs are a parasite of the mind. We, the
human host for a parasite that lives and breeds within us and
spreads through our thought processes, are finally waking up
after centuries of the most diabolical enslavement.

The truth shall set you free. That is my agenda -- and it is our
agenda. Anthony and the heavenly host are dispelling the illu-

sions and teaching us the truth. Your loved ones and ancestors in spirit can teach you the truth too and prove it to you in ways that leave no doubt. You've known since page one that this part was coming. Now I will show you.

YOU CAN CONNECT TOO

We all have the ability to intuitively know things. It's just something you feel or even see. The ability is built-in; intuition is a sixth sense of the nervous system, used to sense energy, and with experience, you learn to trust it. Obi-Wan Kenobi and Yoda from Star Wars repeatedly tell Luke Skywalker to use the Force and trust his feelings. And you might have noticed it takes a while before this lesson sinks in. Trust takes time.

Love and intuition go hand-in-hand. Without love you can go no further, so if you are blocked from your intuition, begin by opening your heart to love. Love is the Force that holds this universe together, present in everything and everyone, and it expresses itself in you through your actions. Remember that. Even if you don't feel love you can express it. You can be it and embody it and give it. After all, love is a verb, and verbs are what? Actions. Your heart is your direct connection to source. The more your heart space is open the clearer your communication can be.

Much can be gained by listening to our inner guidance, the voice of intuition. Learning to connect with a loved one in spirit is no different. Intuition and connection take time and practice but are attainable for everyone.

We learn a new way of living as we open up to our intuitive gifts. For many centuries the information has been suppressed. That control shall be relinquished now as we learn to open up to this wonderful way of living. Each of us is naturally in touch all the time with our higher self, the part of us that exists outside of space-time. There is no separation. But there is a lack of listening.

Each of us is naturally intuitive, too. Some intuitions are transmitted to our conscious minds from our higher self. It's why we sense things we have difficulty putting into words. We just know it to be true because it comes from the ultimate source of truth. Develop your relationship with your higher self and you will be able to communicate directly with it telepathically.

Connecting with Loved Ones in Spirit: the Four "Clairs"

We connect with our loved ones in spirit by using the four primary clair senses: claircognizance, clairsentience, clairvoyance, and clairaudience. These senses, commonly referred to as "sixth sense," parallel our physical senses and are intuitive in nature. You could say they are the senses of the spirit body or soul integrated with the physical body's nervous system and brain.

Claircognizance: the receiving of thoughts and ideas out of "nowhere" (though they are coming from "somewhere"). This sixth sense is related to telepathy and some people do it naturally. Telepathy is a form of communication in thoughts and ideas.

Clairsentience: the intuitive and deeply sensitive feeling of energy and vibrations, or "vibes." A gut feeling can be clairsentient. Empathy can be clairsentient. Strong reactions to negative emotions and sensing a person's true intentions can be clairsentient.

Clairvoyance: the ability to see images or movie-like scenes in your Third Eye. If you are highly clairvoyant you might see images in your physical environment, outside of your Third Eye. You might see colored lights when your eyes are open or closed.

Clairaudient: the hearing of sounds and voices outside of normal hearing range and from sources that aren't physical. You might hear voices originating outside of your body or within your head. Or it could be your own voice speaking to you differently, from a source outside of the physical, i.e. your higher self. People with clairaudient ability might also hear high-pitched sounds or frequencies without knowing why.

The clair senses are all tuned to receive messages from people, and from beings who are not physical, but they are not the only source.

Spirit knows your strengths. It knows which sense is best for reaching you and what's happening in your mind at the time. For example, your mind is distracted by a phone conversation while driving. You come to a traffic light and suddenly feel the urge to slow down. It's so strong you get goosebumps. You slow down just in time to miss colliding with a car that barrels through the intersection.

Heeding your clairsentience saves the day and maybe your life, too. Your mind was too busy at the time for you to be reached with claircognizance, and your ears were too occupied to be reached with clairaudience. Clairvoyance -- a powerful image seen in your mind's eye -- isn't the right sense to use while driving, either. Instead, you have a gut feeling because it's the best way to reach you at the time. For some people it's the best for reaching them anytime because it's the clair sense they know best.

You have a gut feeling that saved you from a car accident, but where does it come from? Something knows the danger as you approach the intersection, and it cares enough to manipulate energy so it's felt by your nervous system. But is it a deceased loved one sending the message? Sometimes. Is it a spirit guide or angel? Sometimes. Other times the source could be precognition -- the previous night you saw the scene in a dream and the sudden deja vu of witnessing it come true jolts you. Or you know better than to drive while distracted and it hit you just in time. Or maybe it's a combination. The rational mind wants a clearly defined cause and effect, but the intuitive mind has no need for it. It just "knows."

I can say for sure that intuitive senses can be developed. And oftentimes you learn to listen because of times when you don't and regret it. Spirit calls that "practice," and the more you practice, the better you get.

You can have many such experiences with clair senses before realizing, for example, that the ringing in your ears you think is tinnitus is actually a loved one in spirit communicating with you in a frequency above normal hearing range. Then you learn to slow down your mind and hear the silence behind the chatter, and the ringing turns into a voice you recognize. Or you see the face of the loved one in your mind's eye. Or you just feel them and their loving presence. There's never anything to fear when they connect with you -- they live in a state of continuous knowledge of complete divine love for everyone. They can never come to you in darkness, pain, or fear.

The source of sudden flashes of inspiration you get could be claircognizance, beamed into your brain from the spirit realm. Nikola Tesla, regarded as one of the most brilliant scientists and whose inventions underpin modern technology, said his inspirations came from a source beyond himself.

> "My brain is only a receiver, in the Universe, there is a core from which we obtain knowledge, strength, and inspiration. I have not penetrated into the secrets of this core, but I know that it exists.
> -Nikola Tesla

Some people do not have access to all the clair senses, and certain senses might be stronger in some people than in others. Find out which is your strongest and run with it.

I teach clients how to open their intuitive abilities as well as learn which clair sense is their strongest. Take your pick from the many exercises. The best clair sense to work on first is the weakest one -- that's usually what spirit guidance tells me to do for my clients. So for example if a client is weakest in the area of clairvoyance, I direct them to candle gaze for 5-10 minutes per day. It decalcifies the pineal gland (seat of the Third Eye) and sharpens our inner vision. With practice you will see the flame split in two and images dancing in the flames.

Connecting with Loved Ones in Spirit: Physical Signs

Spirit can communicate with physical signs as well. Anthony has finalized this chapter by sharing with me amazing physical aspects of his ability to communicate from the spirit world. He still exists and he is capable of defying the laws of physics to show it. This part of the book serves as physical confirmation that spirit very much exists and can be seen and experienced in the material world.

First, Anthony has a message for you, channeled from him to me to you:

The book [of your life] continues.

I died but I live on. I'm not gone. I'm right here with you, existing in a different form. I'm always here, and I know everything [I want to know].

I trust wholeheartedly what Anthony tells me, and although some days I'm at a loss, he reminds me he is here, loud and proud.

Anthony is learning to show his presence physically and having quite the adventure doing it. He first showed himself in the glass beads a friend made from his ashes.

Ivory La Noue, my friend and co-worker has a friend, Brian Fix. Brian makes glass beads with the funerary ashes of loved ones. He asked me if I'd like him to make beads for me and I said sure, how about two beads to go on my necklace. Make them color green, Anthony's favorite color.

Fast-forward a bit. Brian has been working the last few weeks to get the beads done. He does it all the time so this time should be no different, right?

Wrong....

Anthony is not your typical spirit, and I am learning that his way is the way we will be doing things. Just as strong-willed in spirit as he was in physical form, he is teaching me that he can do anything he wishes to show us he is still here.

Brian started making the beads, and every one of them shatters -- more than 15. In all the years he has been making beads from funerary ashes, this has never happened, Brian says.

Is that you Anthony?

I'm not sure. We move along.

Two more weeks of trying to make beads -- green beads -- and Brian throws up his hands and says to Anthony, "Dude, I'm desperate, trying to get these beads made for your mother. Help me out here. What color do you want them?"

Finally the next day he sets out to make some more beads. He hears Anthony say telepathically, "black beads, and make three of them, not two."

Three is a big number for me. That's the second clue Anthony dropped about his presence during the making of the beads. Anthony knows my special number, not Brian.

Brian gets to work quickly, trying to complete the job before Christmas. He makes three black beads with Anthony's ashes and sets them out overnight. He returns in the morning to get the beads and is shocked to find *the beads have turned green.*

The third time's the charm. It's also Anthony's third clue that he physically showed his presence in the making of the beads. There are no coincidences.

According to Brian, beads cannot change color. He's been doing this work for years and is an expert.

They did change color though, to green, Anthony's favorite. Anthony's young love of his life, Kristin, shares a story she remembers about him and the color black. She tells me that Anthony would say black on its own was rather boring, but when you can make it what you want, it becomes beautiful.

He showed himself by making black beautiful and making a statement, too.

Here are the beads pictured with a vial of his ashes.

Confirmation again that spirit is powerful and present. The spirits of our loved ones are here, proud of what they can do now and happy to broadcast it loudly.

I'm still learning that while my son is not physically here with us he does live on in another realm, not just floating around somewhere, but here. Here with us and where he is simultaneously.

I'm still learning it's okay to miss him physically but it's not necessary because he is right here. Ever-present in our lives.

Others have shared stories of their miraculous connection with him in spirit as well. Many people have seen, felt or heard from him again, further confirming that HE IS HERE.

And he is showing others with his presence that your loved ones are here as well.

The next story of Anthony showing his presence material-ly involves a photograph. Spirit can be photographed as light waves or orbs, or there can be an actual physical apparition in windows and glass. Spirit does exist and can be photographed -- it's been done scientifically under controlled conditions. Research from sources such as the Windbridge Institute and the Theosophical Society has proven the existence of spirit. The information is suppressed, and the mind virus we call ra-tional materialism prevents most people from truly absorbing

the information when they encounter it. But the situation is changing.

The following photo was not tampered in any way other than me circling the image. Our family was together celebrating New Years'. My parents, Aunt, and Uncle, and cousins got together for dinner and as a natural occurrence now set a place for Anthony at the table. They set their phone on a tripod with a timer and took a few photos at dinner. This one clearly shows a face in the glass. So compelling, I asked my parents if either of my other sons were there with them because it looked just like my older son. My parents' answer was no, just them.

Again, making it clear and compelling evidence that Anthony attends family functions, as he did when he was with us on Earth. When he made these things available to me it was to show others that spirit does indeed exist and they are quite capable of giving us physical proof. They share in our celebrations and our hardships as well. Always supporting.

Photo is pictured below: It shows Anthony's cousin, Christopher, at a New Years' Eve dinner with my parents and aunt and uncle.

Finally, I have an EVP (Electronic Voice Phenomenon) recording. My first attempts yielded only indistinguishable sounds -- they wouldn't be admitted as evidence in a court of law -- but I continued working on getting one with him speaking clearly and slowly so that I can understand him. It takes quite a bit of energy for them to communicate at times, depending on how they are exerting their energy. They are also learning new ways to use and harness their energy to be able to do many things.

Finally, I worked with someone with experience with EVP and got a clear recording of Anthony. It was so beautiful I began crying immediately. We worked together as I set a sacred container around us. I spent a half-hour clearing and adding spiritual protection around us, then I did a healing on myself and my son to help him bring through the message: "I am sending true love to you." It created this immense energy in my field and body as well. I could feel my ribs being pulled further apart as this bright white emanated from me to him, creating this sacred container.

I held space for another half-hour while working on receiving what was needed. This will be added to my website and facebook page for you to listen to.

Again, I am blown away by the ability of spirit to communicate with us.

Recently I have begun teaching others about the grief process and how to allow the feelings to come through without it taking them down to where they cannot function. Looking in-depth about what they are feeling and expressing that in a way that can help them to heal. I also teach the importance of self-care and energy healing to help in the grief process. I teach others how to open communication with their loved ones through various means. All of these help us to understand that the book still continues and we can still have a loving relationship with our loved ones in spirit

Everyone can learn to connect with spirit. We are all connected whether it is our child, our parent, or our sibling.

Speaking of, Anthony's brother Tyler, aka Toast, found an amazing angel coin in his office at work. He had asked Anthony to send him a sign and his big brother came through for him. This beautiful coin showed up. Out of nowhere it appeared during an especially hard time after Anthony passed.

Spirit comes in when you are having a rough time, whether while grieving or when life gets you down. My entire family has been brought to our knees with the passing of Anthony. Quite frankly, it has brought us closer but has been extremely difficult on everyone. Anthony's grandparents -- my father and mother -- have suffered tremendously, and while they are open to the unknown, their grief can leave them feeling blocked. But Anthony visited them when they needed him the most.

My father was getting ready for bed one night, distraught and crying. Then he felt a pressure around him and the most amazing bear hug ever from Anthony. It brought my father to a place of peace.

My mother experienced a similar situation when she was at home in her bathroom. She bent over, feeling crippling sorrow, and heard a voice, not her own, say, "Everything is going to be OK." She immediately felt content and peaceful as a presence surrounded her. The experience of feeling and hearing her grandson's spirit has been comforting and helped her get through the most difficult times.

Spirit is here and wants to connect with us. They are "out there" in the next life, and they are here too. They enjoy leaving us signs and objects like coins and feathers to find. They can speak through the presence of animals, especially birds and butterflies but also pets. Some people have these experiences and write them off as wishful thinking or delusion. Grief and pain certainly can make you nutty and believe things that aren't true. But when you accept what your heart tells you about the experience of a deceased loved one's visitation it brings relief and healing.

Oftentimes after a loved one passes we just want to know they're OK. Rationalism has deluded us to think death is the end, a belief -- unproven, by the way -- that's contrary to what most people in most times of human history have known to be true. Truth is, the source of life is infinite and eternal, and when we die we go home. We wake up from the dream of life, and once again we experience, 24/7, the divine love that created us. When in spirit, divine love is a fact that just is, and there's no separation. Think of a fish in the water. You are the fish, and the water is divine love. It's a fact of your existence, and to deny it or disbelieve it is simply not possible.

Keep in mind that your deceased loved ones are having a new experience of life, and their ability to connect with people who are in the body varies depending on their development and ability to adjust to their new existence. They might not be ready or able to connect with you, but you can connect with them through your spirit guides and clair senses. Anthony transitioned to his next state of existence and hit the ground running. He did not fear death; he knew his existence would continue. He brought very little baggage with him; his conscience was clear. Most importantly, he brought with him strong bonds of love with his loved ones.

Also keep in mind, the first rule of spirit contact is "do no harm." That means YOU need to be ready and open, too. If a spiritual visitation would rock your boat too hard it won't happen. You can prepare by working through grief and balancing your emotions.

You can meditate. You can take care of yourself. You can open your heart space. And you can assist your loved ones in spirit with your prayers, rituals, and energy work. The road runs both ways. Anthony tells me he will teach us more about how the living can assist and connect with spirit in the next book.

Grief is it can block your ability to connect. Go through the healing process! Healing through grief requires work on your part which I outlined in the chapter on grief. Grief and sorrow are the seeds of new life and beauty. Do the work and feel the feelings from the loss of your loved ones. They are not gone. You only lost the physical part of them.

When teaching students how to connect with spirit, the number one thing I tell them is they must believe. Have faith. You must believe you are powerful enough to have this connection and your loved one is able to communicate. Belief is a bridge to the truth. You know the truth because you experience it, and by believing first (or call it "having faith") you are open to the experience. Truth experienced in this way is no longer belief, it is knowing.

[When Carl Jung was asked by an interviewer if he believed in God, he pondered the question and replied, "Belief is a slippery thing.... I don't need to believe; I know." Dr. Jung had several encounters with spirits from the afterlife.]

Endings and Beginnings

As I close out this book I would like to again say how grateful I am that Anthony is beside me, guiding me in the writing of this book and the journey of this life. These are his words written through me to bring the continuing message that we move on to another realm after leaving the body, still existing and continuing our soul's path. Our relationship as mother and son, as spirit to spirit, continues. So does your relationship with your loved ones, and it can be a conscious, evolving, dynamic relationship if you want it to be (and work at it).

He asks that you continue to increase your awareness not only of your connection with spirit but your connection with self. Remember, movement toward spirit is inward, into the center of your being, and outward simultaneously.

In the coming months and years there is so much to look forward to. Humanity's paradigm is shifting as eternal truths obliterate centuries of lies. Anthony and I and the countless others having these experiences are a growing wave. We teach, show, and prove the connection each of us have to others in our Earth family and our soul group. The day we prove life after death is the day the cage doors swing open.

The next book, for now, titled Life After Death, will explore deeper into subjects introduced in this book: reincarnation and past lives; life in spirit and existence in other dimensions and on other planets; channeling and mediumship. Our family's experience of losing Anthony then getting him back inspired his 10-year old sister Sophia to write a book titled Someone I Love Lives in Heaven, about her feelings, the impact of her grief, and her ongoing relationship with her "Butters," her older brother and guardian angel who is a living presence in her life.

Thank you Anthony Joseph for choosing me to be your mom in this lifetime, and for guiding me on our journey as it continues.

Made in the USA
San Bernardino, CA
30 April 2020

70534856R00091